KG-A

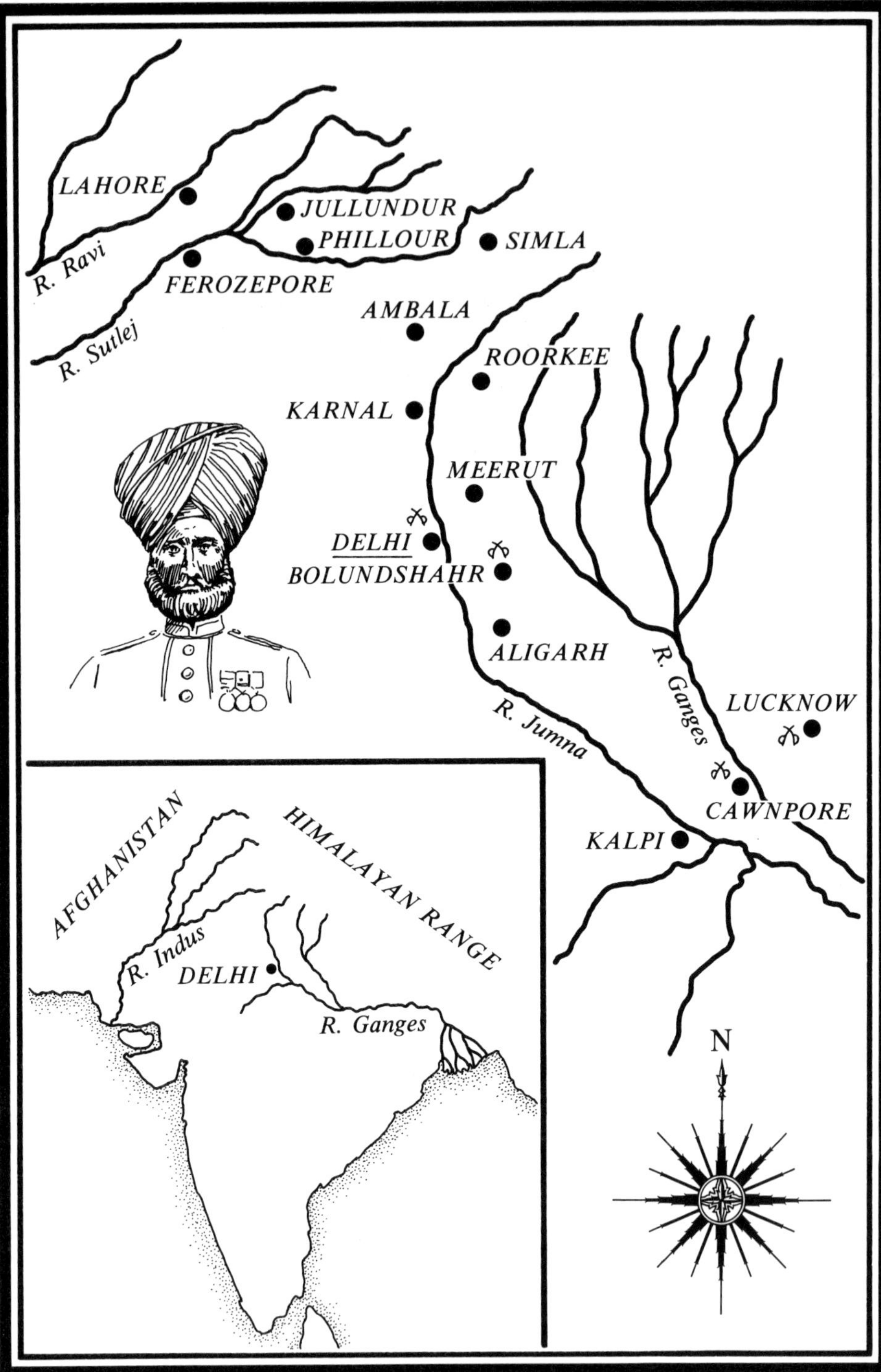

LAHORE
JULLUNDUR
PHILLOUR
SIMLA
R. Ravi
FEROZEPORE
AMBALA
R. Sutlej
ROORKEE
KARNAL
MEERUT
DELHI
BOLUNDSHAHR
ALIGARH
R. Ganges
LUCKNOW
R. Jumna
CAWNPORE
KALPI
AFGHANISTAN
HIMALAYAN RANGE
R. Indus
DELHI
R. Ganges
N

Roger Perkins

Lieutenant Home & the Delhi VCs

PICTON PUBLISHING CHIPPENHAM
1983

by the same Author

THE PUNJAB MAIL MURDER
The story of an Indian Army Officer

GUNFIRE IN BARBARY
Admiral Lord Exmouth and the
Battle of Algiers, 1816
(with Capt K J Douglas-Morris RN)

First published by Picton Publishing (Chippenham) Ltd 1983
ISBN 0 902633 87 2

Photoset in 10/12 Times Roman
by Chippenham Typesetting, Bath Road, Chippenham, Wiltshire
Text paper supplied by Howard Smith Papers, Bristol.
Bound by J. W. Braithwaite & Sons Ltd, Wolverhampton
Printed in Great Britain by Picton Print
Citadel Works, Bath Road, Chippenham, Wiltshire.

Contents

Foreword

The recent battles of the Falkland Islands have given us a vivid reminder of the qualities of courage and sacrifice which win a Victoria Cross. It is the supreme award for gallantry in the face of the enemy.

Duncan Home – in the early days when the Honourable East India Company was responsible for law and order in India – was one of the first to be decorated for such valour.

This dramatic account of his successful mission to blow up the Kashmir Gate, and so allow the British forces to capture Delhi, was an exploit of high daring undertaken with no thought whatever for his own safety.

There are moving accounts of his personal leadership by contemporaries who saw his triumph and his death.

The Kashmir Gate act of bravery had a lasting significance, for, as the author claims, it laid the foundation for the years of successful government by Britain through the Indian Civil Service, one of the greatest administrative services of all time.

The Right Honourable The Lord Home of The Hirsel, KT
The House of Lords, Palace of Westminster
December 1982

Notes & Acknowledgements

This book has its origins in two military campaign medals which I acquired for my collection in 1982. The Punjab medal and the Mutiny medal are both handsome examples of the engraver's art. Even to someone having no particular interest in such matters, these heavy disks of Victorian silver, suspended from their distinctive ribbons, are aesthetically pleasing. From the standpoint of the military researcher, however, they possess the added merit of having been issued with the recipient's name upon the lower rim.

A first inspection of these two medals revealed that they had upon their rims the name of Lieutenant D C Home of the Bengal Engineers. Enquiries quickly confirmed the important and exciting fact that this officer had been awarded the Victoria Cross. Sadly, over the years, the Cross became separated from the two campaign medals and, at the time of writing, it still cannot be traced. Nevertheless, I was pleased to assume the stewardship of such historically significant items and I am grateful to his great grand-niece, Mrs Margaret Home-Tucker, for having granted me this role.

I was equally pleased to have a reason for researching the background story to the awards. I soon discovered that it is a very good story, full of courage, drama and human interest. I also rediscovered the old truth – one cannot compile a research dossier without the unstinted support of fellow collectors and the advice of specialists in other fields. Thanks to the flow of information received from a large number of friends (old and new), what began as a private collector's file on Duncan Home has grown into a somewhat longer narrative which, hopefully, will reach a wider readership than otherwise would have been the case.

I am indebted to the following institutions and organisations for having so generously granted access to their archives: India Office Library & Records, National Army Museum, National Portrait Gallery, British Association for Cemeteries in South Asia, Military History Society, Royal Greenjackets Museum, Manchester Central Registry, Manchester

Local History Museum, Dorset County Records Office, Public Record Office (Kew), and the National Maritime Museum.

Of the many individuals who have given enthusiastic advice, particular mention must be made of the Reverend Canon W M Lummis MC. He developed his interest in the Victoria Cross in 1895 at the age of nine. Now approaching his centenary, he has amassed from a variety of sources a wealth of archival references to VC winners. At least two of the important private letters quoted in this book would have been lost to us if Canon Lummis had not maintained his life-time habit of conservation. Many of the biographical details listed in Appendix J are also the fruit of his endeavours.

For their editorial suggestions, based upon their intimate knowledge of India, I am grateful to Major Robin Hodson and Sir Torquil Matheson of Matheson. My neighbour, Max Powling, has been unfailingly helpful in tracing bibliograpical sources. I am similarly indebted to Ian and Ronald Baxter, who have an encylopaedic knowledge of India's history; to David Morris and Major Eric Leask, for their expertise in the history of the Oxfordshire & Buckinghamshire Light Infantry; to Henry Lloyd, who was himself a sapper officer in India; to Theon and Rosemarie Wilkinson, who have done so much to record and preserve the memorials of the Raj; and to Keith Northover for his meticulous work in checking *The London Gazette* entries.

I am also glad to record the invaluable support of Dennis Pillinger, Paul Lewis, Major Peter Abbot RA, Lionel Digby, Major Alan Harfield R Sigs, A Brandon-Langley, Carol Blackett-Ord, Stewart Murphy, Pauline Rohatgi, Patricia Kattenhorn, Mildred Archer, Robert E Salkeld, Roy and Vera Salkeld, Charles Townsend, Zoë Yalland, Richard Humble, Julie Lamara, Rev Gilbert Russell, Rev Roger Bagnall, Lieutenant Colonel A M Macfarlane RA, Major General B P Hughes CB CBE, Laurie Manton, David Picton-Phillips BSc, and Mike Wicks.

The book is embellished by the skills of three people who share my interest in military research: Bob Scarlett produced the crystal-clear medal photographs, John Blanche designed the dust-jacket, and Kenneth Petrie (a medal collector in Maryland USA) has based his portraits of Home, Salkeld and Hawthorne upon the few murky pictures which have survived the past one hundred and twenty-five years.

The two fine maps are the work of Brian Ainsworth, an old friend and near neighbour.

One of the dilemmas identified in correspondence with my helpers was the preferred spelling of certain Indian ranks, titles, and place-names. Over the past two centuries there have been numerous changes in the manner in which the British have sought to express, phonetically and in Roman characters, the euphony of the languages of India. An obvious example occurs in the title of this book. During the period when these events took place, the conventional spelling was Cashmere.

There are other instances where one is faced with a choice: Umritsur versus Amritsar, Bhurtpoor versus Bhurtpore, Peshawur versus Peshawar. Similarly, one encounters Hindoo and Hindu, Goorkha and Gurkha, Naick and Naik. At the risk of offending the purist, I have chosen in the main to follow the modern usages except in those instances where the word is found within a quotation from a nineteenth century source.

A parallel problem may be identified in the pronunciation of Duncan Home's surname. It is well known that the author of the Foreword to this book, the Lord Home, formerly Sir Alec Douglas Home, Prime Minister of Great Britain, is correctly addressed only when the pronunciation rhymes with 'spume'. This particularity is a reflection of the various spellings encountered in the early written records: Home, Hume, Hwm and Hoome. The practice followed by Duncan's branch of the family is that the name should rhyme with 'dome'.

A selected bibliography appears at the end of this book which is intended as a general guide to those who may wish to study in depth the story of the Great Sepoy Mutiny and the siege of Delhi. Reference to these sources will show, however, that there are discrepancies between the previously published accounts. It is perhaps inevitable that this should be so, some of the stories having been written many years after the Mutiny when memories were no longer fresh. As a matter of principle, I have relied primarily upon official reports published by authority, and upon eyewitness accounts written during the battle and in its immediate aftermath.

Even so, it is not always easy to establish the precise facts. The circumstances surrounding the death of Captain Douglas at Delhi, on 11 May 1857, provide a classic illustration of the dilemma. Two apparently authoritative Indian writers, both of whom were present in the city, wrote widely differing accounts of his wounding and subsequent murder. In the final analysis, the quality of truth is sometimes a matter of personal interpretation.

Appendix A of this volume is a brief summary of the manner in which the Victoria Cross was awarded to Duncan Home and some of his contemporaries at Delhi. However, this is a large and complex subject. It is dealt with, in its entirety and in a most erudite style, in *The Evolution of the Victoria Cross – a Study in Administration*, by the late M J Crook. His book is recommended reading for the specialist.

Finally, it is my hope that *The Kashmir Gate* will win the approval of fellow collectors and historians, and that it may be useful to them in their own researches. More importantly, however, I hope that the story will be of interest to the general reader, and that he or she may judge the book to be a fitting memorial to a group of men whose lives were far removed from our own experience.

Over a period of nearly 350 years, the British enjoyed the privilege of a very special relationship with the peoples of India. Despite the frustrations and conflicts which inevitably arise from such a close encounter between two entirely different cultural and religious heritages, the historical co-involvement was one which enriched the lives and understanding of both parties. It is not possible to separate the history of Great Britain from the history of India, they are too closely intermingled. In the closing years of the twentieth century, an entire generation of young Britons has grown to adulthood with little comprehension of the powerful forces which in former years bound together the destinies of two countries, six thousand miles apart.

White skin or brown, there has been a long-running mutuality of interests into which the tragedy of 1857 came as a short-lived aberration. Perhaps the current resurgence of interest in the life story of one of India's greatest sons, Mahatma Gandhi, is indicative of a hidden but deep-rooted awareness that our two peoples still have much to learn from each other.

Introduction

Since the date of its inception, one thousand three hundred and fifty-one men, of many creeds and colours, have been awarded the Victoria Cross. Of all the medals and decorations ever conferred by the monarch or government of any country, the VC is the most readily recognised and the most easily understood. Even for the civilian who might otherwise have little interest in matters medallic or military, this simple piece of bronze has a special significance.

By the same token, the names of certain individuals awarded the VC have become firmly implanted in the folk-memory of the English-speaking peoples. Only the very young may not be familiar with the exploits of heroes upon whom the full limelight of twentieth century publicity has shone. The mere mention of 'Boy' Cornwell, Guy Gibson, Leonard Cheshire, Bill Speakman, James Carne, 'H' Jones, and many others, is sufficient to evoke an instant mental image.

It is when we attempt to look further back in time, back to the reign of the Queen whose name the medal bears, that the power of memory is more sternly tested. Who today can recall the soldiers and sailors who achieved this ultimate distinction while serving in almost every corner of the globe during the second half of the nineteenth century? A few names come quickly to mind: Charles Lucas, 'Bobs' Roberts, the Gough brothers, Bromhead and Chard, perhaps a few others. But not many. They are wraiths, misty figures marching across the silent wastes of yesteryear's battlefields.

Even for the specialist student, it is not easy to bring the stories of these men into sharper focus. Too many of the written records – the daily diaries and the letters home to friends and family – have been lost to us. The eyewitnesses, the comrades-in-arms who were present at the moment of glory, are all long gone. Too often we are left with nothing more than the dry official account, the dusty archive, which tells the story only in part.

The following pages do not purport to offer a complete analysis of the causes and effects of the Great Sepoy Mutiny of 1857–9. Other pens, far better qualified, have dealt with this task in past years. The intention here is simply that of giving a human dimension to the individual stories of just four men – three Englishmen and an Irishman – who gained the supreme award for valour more than a century ago. In the space of a few mad moments, before the walls of India's capital city, they displayed those qualities which are common to all recipients of the Cross. We have witnessed the same qualities again, in the recent past, in the South Atlantic war.

The four took part in the most remarkable event of the Mutiny – the attack at the Kashmir Gate, Delhi, on 14 September 1857. They set off an explosion which demolished this principal entrance to the fortified city. Their success permitted the main assault force to gain entry, to get to grips with the enemy, and eventually to recapture a place which was, and still is, the symbol of power and authority for the whole of India.

If they had failed, then the main assault, in all probability, would have failed also. The attackers were few, their opponents numerous, the margins of error non-existent. But they did not fail and, once Delhi was returned to British control, the final bloody suppression of the Mutiny in other cities was assured. The explosion at the Kashmir Gate was the turning point. The pillar of black smoke climbing into the pale blue sky signalled the moment of advance for the attacking columns. With hindsight, however, it can be seen that it is also heralded a further ninety years of a continuing British presence in India. It is for this reason that the names of the four leading participants – Home, Salkeld, Smith and Hawthorne – merit the attention to which this volume is devoted.

The attack was planned and commanded by Lieutenant Duncan Charles Home of the Bengal Engineers. It was his quality of leadership, his willingness to be the first man to go forward, which inspired his comrades. The central theme of the following account, therefore, is the story of his life and times.

THE KASHMIR GATE

India, 1857. For the first time in many years, the 300 million polyglot peoples of the huge sub-continent found themselves living under the protection of a single authority. The Honourable East India Company, until 1833 a semi-autonomous trading company, had assumed control of almost one quarter of the world's entire population. Known more comfortably as John Company, its Board of Control had achieved, almost by accident, that which others had failed to do. It had brought the rule of law, and an expectation of stability, to people who formerly had rarely experienced either.

The British first reached the coast of Southern India (Malabar and Coromandel) at the close of the sixteenth century. They sought nothing more than trade, most particularly the purchase of the many spices which are the produce of that part of the world. Limiting themselves intially to tiny toe-hold enclaves on the coastal plains, they later became embroiled in the complex politics of the hinterland. The British needed also to keep a wary eye on the commercial and territorial ambitions of other European maritime nations.

To ensure their commercial security, to afford protection to those Indians who turned to them for support, the John Company administrators found it necessary to raise a private army. With time this force grew in size and stature until, by the middle of the nineteenth century, it had carried the tide of John Company rule northwards to the forbidding borders of Persia, Afghanistan and Tibet. The failing power of the Islamic Mogul Empire had been swept away and even the mighty warrior races – the Mahrattas, the Sikhs and the Gurkhas – had declared their allegiance to the British. Peace and good order had been established in the span of only a few decades. The worst legacies of former despotic rulers were disappearing, the construction of a major road and railway system was proceeding apace, civil and criminal justice was being dispensed by men of high quality. From the complacent British point of view, every prospect pleased and the future of India seemed assured. Then came disaster.

The root causes of the Great Mutiny were many and complex. To the nineteenth century Englishman it was a terrible betrayal of trust. To a twentieth century Indian it was a genuine war of independence. Even today this is a controversial and emotional subject. However, by popular consensus, the catalyst was the issue of a new type of firearm to the John Company soldiery. Conceived in England by people who were unaware (or uncaring) of the tenets of the Muslim and Hindu religions, the cartridges for the new Enfield rifle needed to be coated with a protective layer of wax. Earlier types of cartridge were similarly coated – with coconut oil and beeswax – but this new material was alleged to contain a proportion of cow tallow, odious to Hindus of every caste. Possibly also it contained pig fat, equally abhorrent to the followers of Muhammad. Already unsettled by the swift pace of the Company's legal, economic and social reforms, the sepoys were ready to believe that the new cartridges presented a deliberate threat to their religious integrity. Agitators told the troops that the British were determined to defile them before converting them forcibly to the alien faith of Christianity. The accusation was unfounded, but many Indians became very alarmed and the British response was less then adroit.

The first serious incident occurred in March, 1857, at Barrackpore, a few miles north of Calcutta. A sepoy of the 34th Native Infantry, one Manghal Pandi, attacked a British officer and tried to kill him while the regimental quarter guard stood passively watching. Order was restored and Manghal Pandi was hanged. When later the full storm of mutiny swept through other native regiments, the name of this soldier became a rallying cry. To the mutineers he was a martyr; to the British troops sent to suppress them he provided a title which they applied to all mutineers – 'the Pandis'.

The 34th Regiment was quietly disbanded, and several other regiments also. But disaffection spread like wildfire from cantonment to cantonment, up the valley of the Ganges, until the loyalty of many native regiments was trembling on the knife edge. The bonds of that loyalty were finally cut at Meerut, forty miles north-east of the capital city of Delhi. Following an incident when eighty-five sepoys had been manacled and jailed after refusing the new cartridges, three regiments suddenly rose in blind fury against their British officers. In one night of horror they butchered a large number of British men, women and children.

It was the beginning of the greatest tragedy ever to afflict any country to which Great Britain had brought a benign colonialism. There was fault on both sides, but the British were largely the authors of their own misfortune. Many decades were to pass before the scars of the Great Sepoy Mutiny could heal, and even today they are still apparent. The

Sepoys of the 5th Bengal Native Infantry at rifle practice and apparently discussing the cartridges which they so distrusted. (India Office Library & Records)

names of two Indian cities in particular still evoke memories of terrible suffering and great bravery – Lucknow and Cawnpore. And the names of the senior British officers and administrators who, during the following months, struggled to contain and suppress the revolt, still shine brightly. James Outram, Henry Havelock, the Lawrence brothers, John Nicholson, Colin Campbell – these were some of the senior men who strove to repair the damage.

But there were many younger men, officers of lower rank and far less experience, who met the challenge of the occasion and whose names are remembered for the resource and courage which they displayed. One of these was a 29-years-old Lieutenant of the Bengal Army, Duncan Charles Home. The final weeks of his short life were, by any standard, extraordinary.

Duncan Home was born on 10 June, 1828, at Jubbulpore, Central Provinces. His father was Major General Richard Home of the Bengal Army, an officer who had seen much service during the campaigns for the conquest of Northern India (as had his brother, Major General John Home). The family had extensive branches in England and Scotland, and

The British could not hope to control the Punjab without first occupying the southern city of Mooltan. Its fortress and armaments were at that time immensely powerful and, being located near the confluence of the Indus, Chenab and Sutlej rivers, it effectively dominated the line of march of any army attempting to invade from the south. The British besieged the place twice, from July to September 1848 and again from September through to January 1849. As so often on this and similar occasions, the Bengal Engineers took the leading role in planning and constructing the elaborate siege works. Duncan Home played his part during the weeks preceding the assault on 2 January and witnessed the violence of the clash when the assaulting columns advanced through the breaches in the city walls. (Oil painting by Henry Martens, India Office Library & Records)

it produced a number of men who rose to high rank in the service of India.

Young Duncan was sent back to Europe at the age of eight. India's climate and diseases caused high mortality amongst the children of British families and it was the custom to send them home at an early age to be educated. Duncan was a boarder first at Elizabeth College, Guernsey, and later at Staton's School, Wimbledon. He then went on to the Honourable East India Company's Military Seminary at Addiscombe, near Croydon (Surrey). He passed out at the head of his class in December 1846. After a further period of military training at the engineering establishment at Chatham he sailed for India in July 1848. He had secured a commission as Second Lieutenant in the Bengal Engineers and, with all the enthusiasm of a 19-years-old newly accoutred subaltern, he looked forward to returning to the land of his birth.

At that time the British and HEIC armies both still followed the peculiar practice of having two separate engineer organisations, one for officers and another for other ranks. Hence, in the British Army, officers were members of the Royal Corps of Engineers while the men served with the Royal Corps of Sappers & Miners. In the case of Duncan Home and his contemporaries, they were officers of the Bengal Engineers and commanded Indian troops (with a small number of British non-commissioned officers) of the Bengal Sappers & Miners. This anachronism ended after the Mutiny when officers and other ranks were brought together in unified Corps.

Duncan's ship reached Bombay in October. Within a very few days he found himself on a train heading north towards the Upper Provinces. His orders stated that he was to join the staff of General Whish, the officer commanding the forces surrounding the city of Mooltan. Duncan had arrived in India, by chance, in the early stages of what came to be known as the Second Sikh War.

Three years earlier, after a lightning campaign, British and John

Company forces had defeated the 100,000-strong Sikh army in a series of major battles (at Moodkee, Ferozeshuhur, Aliwal and Sobraon). The terms of the peace treaty signed at Lahore left the Sikhs with their own army and with a considerable degree of autonomy in their homeland, the Punjab, but various important political powers were conceded to the British. The latter had no wish to annex yet more territory; they hoped to manipulate Sikh affairs by diplomacy rather than by military occupation. This arrangement was never satisfactory and, in 1848, it broke down.

The Sikhs, still resentful after their defeats during the earlier war, rebelled against the terms imposed upon them. They murdered the British Resident at Mooltan, took over the city, brought together a large army with a powerful force of artillery, and dared the British to do their worst. Delhi responded by sending a mixed force of British and Indian regiments, commanded by Lord Gough, to annex the whole of the Punjab.

Nearly twenty thousand men, led by General Whish, marched to Mooltan and besieged the city from September 1848 to January 1849. On the 22nd of that month the defenders capitulated, but British elation was tempered by the fearful losses which they had suffered only one week earlier at Chilianwala. There, two hundred miles to the north-east, a British force had been roughly handled by a division of Sikh rebels; it was an action which became notorious for the weakness of the British generalship and the near annihilation of the 24th (2nd Warwickshire) Regiment of Foot.

Duncan completed his long journey north by horse and river-boat. His precise duties during his first weeks at Mooltan are not known. He was young and totally without experience. After many years in England his grasp of Indian languages was inadequate for the command of native troops. No doubt he was taken under the wing of a senior subaltern and given minor tasks and responsibilities. Under the pressure of active warfare he must have matured quickly, gaining in confidence and making himself useful to the Chief Field Engineer, Major Robert Napier (later Lord Napier of Magdala). The hazards of the campaign are made clear by one of Duncan's brother officers who described a minor episode during the siege:

> 'Major Napier came over one night. We sat under the awning of my tent with our feet on a table. Lake (Lt E J Lake of the Bengal Engineers) was fast asleep in bed under the same awning. Presently a shot buried itself hissing in the sand by Napier's side; then another ripped its way past me. A third fell at the head of Lake's bed and his servant immediately turned the bed around. Lake asked sleepily "What's the matter?" "Nothing, Sahib", replied the bearer, "only a cannon-ball". So Lake went to sleep again. Five minutes later another shot fell at his feet. Again the good bearer shifted his master's bed and again Lake murmured "What's the matter now?" and was told "Another cannon-ball, nothing more", upon which he said "Oh!" and returned calmly to the land of dreams while Napier and I finished our conversation.'

The final weeks of the campaign were characterised by swift movement across difficult country with numerous interruptions to deal with skirmishers. The sappers marched mainly with the heavy artillery, helping the gunners to move their pieces across rivers and broken ground, but frequently they fought as infantry. Duncan Home's introduction to his new career was comprehensive and intense: the experience was to stand him in good stead eleven years later. It was during this period that he came to know (and be known by) the three officers whom he later served so well at Delhi: John Nicholson, Richard Baird Smith and Alexander Taylor. All three were destined to find their place in the pages of India's history.

One month after the fall of Mooltan came the third and final test of strength between the two sides. The victors of Mooltan, under General Whish, joined forces with the survivors of Chilianwala, under Lord Gough, and together they met the Sikh army at Goojerat. The Sikhs had been reinforced by a large number of Afghan cavalry, but Gough had increased his firepower with more heavy guns. He used his artillery to deadly effect, his infantry advanced in the centre and his cavalry swept

The obverse of the Punjab medal bears the classic profile of Her Majesty designed by William Wyon. The medal was issued without clasp, or with one or two of the three authorised clasps: 'Mooltan', 'Chilianwala' and 'Goojerat'. Due to the dates when the actions took place, and the distances involved, it is not feasible that anyone could have qualified for both of the two first-named clasps. Duncan Home received the clasps shown here. The ribbon is dark blue, with yellow stripes and a narrow blue outer edge. (Photographs by Robert J Scarlett)

The reverse of the Punjab medal was designed by William Wyon and is perhaps one of his most interesting works. After their defeat at Goojerat, the Sikh troops were pursued by 12,000 British and Indian infantry and cavalry under General Sir Walter Gilbert. On 12 March 1849 he obliged them to surrender unconditionally. Wyon's engraving shows the Sikh leaders laying down their arms in submission to the mounted British general under the respectful gaze of his paraded troops. This innovative medal was the first to reflect admiration for a defeated foe.

around both flanks of the Sikh position. It was an overwhelming defeat for the Sikhs: they lost two thousand dead and all their guns. The remainder fled and twenty thousand eventually surrendered.

Duncan Home served as an additional officer on General Whish's staff at Mooltan, and with 3rd Company, Bengal Sappers & Miners, at Goojerat. Subsequently he received the Punjab campaign medal with two

clasps. Lord Gough secured his own special memento of the campaign: he received from the leader of the Sikhs the fabulous *Koh-i-noor* (Mountain of Light) diamond which, at that time, weighed 800 carats! Some years later it was presented to Queen Victoria and incorporated in the Royal regalia.

In March 1849, at the conclusion of the campaign, Duncan was sent to Lahore. The occupation of the Punjab was creating an immense volume of work for the new masters. Apart from establishing a completely new administration, the British commenced an ambitious programme of road and canal construction. They were now on the borders of Afghanistan, standing guard near the traditional gateway for foreign invaders, the Khyber Pass. Efficient communications would be vital if further incursions by the Afghans (or possibly by the Russians) were to be discouraged. The Bengal Engineers, with the Bengal Sappers & Miners, were much involved in this work.

Duncan must have made a favourable impression upon his commanding officer during the few months he served with the 3rd Company because, in October 1849, he obtained one of the sought-after appointments with the Department of Public Works. He became Assistant Executive Officer at Aligarh. His task was that of supervising the construction of a section of the new Ganges Canal. This was his job for the next three years. Then, in April 1852, he was appointed Assistant to the

An 1863 view of the Ganges Canal at Roorkee, set against the spectacularly beautiful back-drop of the Himalayan mountains. Apart from their functional value, public works of this type are monuments to the imagination and determination of their creators. Over a period of many decades, the military engineers laboured to build an extensive network of canals throughout the Indus and Ganges valleys. (Watercolour by William Simpson, India Office Library & Records)

Executive Engineer at Malikpore where the Bari Doab canal was under construction. Twelve months later he was given charge of a complete section of this canal, at Madhopore. It was an immense project, cutting across the area where Gough and Whish had fought their battles with the Sikhs only a few years earlier. Apart from its military value, the canal was intended to improve the lot of the local people by providing water for irrigation and reducing the scale of the monsoon floods.

Duncan is said to have performed his duties 'with great diligence and credit'. He worked throughout these years as a civil engineer rather than as a military man. He had parted company from the Sappers & Miners at Lahore. He was now supervising a large workforce of locally recruited civilian labourers. These people were mainly Muzbee Sikhs, men of the lowest Hindu caste or, in many cases, 'untouchables'. Possessing neither land nor social standing, they welcomed the chance to improve their lot in life through regular work and steady pay. The Muzbees were the descendants of *t'ug* families which traditionally had earned their living by highway robbery and murder. Many aspired to acceptance within the Hindu religion by settling to an honest and respectable trade. Like most Sikhs, they were physically big, cheerful and industrious, and well suited to the heavy work. Duncan remained at Madhopore for the next five years and seems to have enjoyed his time there. He was promoted to the rank of Lieutenant in February 1854.

In June 1857, the routine of his life was broken by the arrival at Madhopore of an urgent telegraph signal from the Chief Commissioner at Lahore. Addressed to the Superintendent of Canals, Lieutenant J H Dyas, Bengal Engineers, it ordered him to raise three companies of Pioneers and send them with all haste to Delhi, two hundred and fifty miles to the south-east. Experienced labourers were needed urgently to build siege works around the city. The capital had been taken over by the mutineers: they had murdered many of the European residents and driven out the survivors. The British had hurriedly formed a force of Crown and loyal native regiments to partially surround the place and recapture it. This would involve a prolonged and elaborate siege operation – hence the call to Madhopore.

Dyas delegated his most experienced subordinate, Duncan Home, to

Men of one of the British regiments on the march south from the Punjab to join the Delhi Field Force. The sick and injured were able to ride part of the way, or be carried in a litter or 'dhooli' as shown here. (India Office Library & Records)

select 240 of his best men and to form them into three companies of eighty men each. Priority was given to the selection of those with previous military experience and who could be trusted with firearms. Within forty-eight hours the job was done and the column was on the road to Phillaur under the temporary command of a Sergeant Robson. At Phillaur the column was issued with side-arms and ammunition and sent on its way down the Grand Trunk Road towards Delhi. They were now led by Lieutenant H W Gulliver, Bengal Engineers, and they reached the outskirts of Delhi in only two weeks.

During that time they fought off a series of mutineer ambushes, in one of which the unfortunate Robson was killed. They acquired a number of bullock carts and 200 camels along the way and, although still lacking uniforms, they marched into the British lines full of confidence and fighting spirit. The staff gave them the provisional title 'Punjab Sappers' (also 'Punjab Pioneers'), and it is interesting to note that this small crowd of Muzbee Sikhs, amongst the lowest in their religious hierarchy and notorious for their criminal antecedents, were the founder-members of what was to become one of the most famous formations in the Indian Army – the Corps of Sikh Pioneers.

The commander of the British forces beseiging Delhi (the Delhi Field Force) was Brigadier General Archdale Wilson. Residing at Meerut when the Mutiny first broke out there, he was regarded by many as a supine and ineffectual officer. Unfortunately he had been serving under Major General W H Hewitt, GOC Meerut Division, a fat old man who, after fifty years of uninterrupted service in India, was incapable of deviating from the set routine of garrison life. Hewitt did nothing to quell the outbreak at Meerut, nor to prevent the mutineers from marching south and

1859: the Mutiny is over, and sick, exhausted and wounded British officers can at last withdraw to the healthier environment of the hill stations to rest and recuperate. The record states that this photograph was taken at Simla and that all four men were officers of the Bengal Engineers, but only one of them has been identified with certainty. The central figure, in the check shirt, is Lieutenant J H Dyas. He was Duncan Home's immediate superior in May 1857, when they were both employed at Madhopore on the construction of the Bari Doab canal, and it was he who ordered Duncan to raise the Muzbee companies and to lead two of them to Delhi. (India Office Library & Records)

spreading the flames to Delhi. Wilson had looked to him for leadership but, failing to find it, had taken the initiative into his own hands. It was a brave move for a man of his hesitant disposition (and still recovering from an attack of smallpox). He had led a small column to Delhi to join the main British force and now, almost by accident, found himself commanding the entire operation. Apart from occasional lapses into depression and self-doubt, Wilson showed signs of becoming a forceful and determined commander.

Some of his staff were well aware of the bad reputation attaching to the Muzbees and doubted whether they were dependable. Wilson over-rode their objections when he saw what Duncan had been able to do, and the quality of the men whom Gulliver had brought with him. Orders were sent to Lahore and Amritsar for the raising of two more Muzbee companies of Punjab Sappers. The task was given to a civil engineer in the Public Works Department, a Russian Pole by the name of Gustiavinski. Granted a temporary commission in the rank of Ensign, he was soon on the long road to Delhi.

Similar orders went to Madhopore where Duncan Home was waiting impatiently for the call to action. Like every other officer in India, he had only one ambition – to get into the fight and throw the Pandis out of the capital city. Dyas was ordered to raise six more companies from his work-force, but he told Duncan to concentrate on raising just two and to then leave as quickly as he could. The message from Delhi stated that Gulliver had been taken ill and, as one of the most experienced junior officers in the Bengal Engineers, Duncan was required to replace him as commander of all the Punjab Sapper companies around the city.

With the mobilisation order came news which was personally distressing to the young officer. The Resident Commissioner at Delhi at the time of the outbreak was Simon Fraser. He was Duncan's uncle and a good friend. The reports now reaching Madhopore stated that Fraser was dead, one of the many victims of the initial blood-letting on the streets of India's capital.

When the mutineers from Meerut were first reported on the outskirts of Delhi, early on 11 May, Fraser had gone with several other European officials to the eastern walls of the city to assess the situation for himself. He was shocked to find the toll-house by the Jumna pontoon-bridge already in flames. Worse, the vanguard of the Pandi column was flooding across the bridge and into the streets, shouting and firing indiscriminately. One of Fraser's companions, Captain Douglas, captain of the guard at the Royal Palace, was shot in the foot. Fraser took shelter in a watch-tower as a party of yelling troopers of the 3rd Cavalry, in their distinctive French-grey uniforms, cantered up to the startled Scotsmen.

The Commissioner found an ancient musket – abandoned by the watchman – and used it to kill one of the cavalrymen before fleeing for his life. Jumping into his trap, he drove quickly through the tumult of the streets to the Royal Palace and there tried to rouse the King's staff to action. Failing, he called on the King's bodyguard – a full company of sepoys – to close the outer gates and to shoot any intruders. Bewildered and frightened, they did nothing. Within minutes, a mob of yelling hooligans – waving swords, knives and iron-bound staves – came pouring into the courtyard. Fraser faced them, alone and unarmed. He tried to address them, to calm their frenzy, but it was hopeless. He turned to climb the steps leading to Captain Douglas's private apartment, where the wounded Captain and several other Europeans had taken refuge, and was instantly struck down. Two *badmashis* – backstreet petty criminals of the type always ready to stir discontent – ran forward and slashed at the Commissioner with long knives. Fraser died under a flurry of cuts and stabs. He was one of the many victims whom the besiegers of Delhi were now determined to avenge.

Fraser's murderers were named Karlik Beg and Mogul Beg. These names were reported to the besieging British forces by their spies within the city. It was assumed – incorrectly – that Mogul Beg was Prince Mogul Beg, nephew of the King of Delhi and one of the squabbling pack of princes who seized upon the mutiny as a chance to further their own interests. The murderer was instead a common ruffian, but the identical names may have had some influence upon the post-battle treatment of the captured princes. Duncan Home, certainly, was convinced that his uncle had been butchered by the old King's nephew.

Duncan arrived with his two companies at Delhi on 20 August, more or less at the same time as Gustiavinski was arriving with his force from Lahore. Both parties had made forced marches of up to thirty miles each night in conditions of extreme heat and heavy rain. Like Gulliver before them, they had received muskets *en route* at the Phillaur arsenal, but each Muzbee was dressed in his travel-stained civilian working clothes and they more resembled a band of bearded cut-throat brigands than a John Company regiment.

The siege works at Delhi were under the overall command of 38-years-old Colonel Richard Baird Smith who, until a short time before, had been Senior Instructor of the Engineering College at Roorkee. Baird Smith, however, was in poor health and much of the day-to-day work was done by Captain Alexander Taylor, the man who had been building the Grand Trunk Road from the Sutlej to Peshawar.

Duncan reported himself to Taylor and was briefed regarding the progress of the battle. For nearly two months the British had been engaged in a series of fierce actions with the outlying Pandi defences and had gradually driven them back into the confines of the city walls. The toughest fight had been for possession of 'the Ridge', a long low hill running north to south which guarded the western approaches to the city. It was now in British hands and had been fortified with cannon and infantry entrenchments. It was too far from the city for the gunners to be able to concentrate their fire and blast a breach in the city walls, but its occupation did prevent the mutineers from bringing in reinforcements from the west. The Ridge position also provided a firm base from which the British could push forward and build new batteries for the heavy siege guns which, hopefully, would bring the walls tumbling down.

It was for this work, building the batteries, that Duncan Home's force was so urgently needed. His tough and work-hardened Muzbees were the only men available to General Wilson who could do such work. The British troops – the 6th Dragoon Guards, 9th Lancers, 8th, 52nd, 60th, 61st, 75th of Foot, 1st and 2nd Bengal Fusiliers – were totally unfitted for heavy manual work in that climate, and they were in any event already badly weakened by cholera, typhoid and heat exhaustion.

Wilson had a considerable number of Bengal and Punjab cavalry and infantry regiments in his force, but their loyalty had been severely strained

The panorama looking south from the Ridge towards the city of Delhi (lost in the heat haze on the right-hand of the horizon). In the foreground, the remains of the British batteries and entrenchments. To the upper left, Sir Theophilus Metcalfe's house (where Philip Salkeld and his companions hid after their escape). On the left-hand horizon, the pale band of the Jumna river. (India Office Library & Records)

by recent events. He could not be certain that they would obey if told to go forward and work under the deluge of musketry, grapeshot and cannon-balls which fell on anyone approaching the city fortifications. He told Baird Smith and Taylor to give the job to Duncan Home and his rag-tag of canal diggers.

During the last week of August the engineer officers were involved in a number of preparatory tasks: cutting down trees and scrub to open up fields of fire for the guns, gathering brushwood to manufacture fascines and gabions (tools of siege work dating from medieval times), floating logs down the Jumna river and hauling them forward to build causeways and revetments. In this work they were aided by the regular troops of the Bengal Sappers & Miners, 129 of whom had remained loyal to the British when the Mutiny first exploded. But the amateurs of Duncan's force also made several armed raids deep into enemy territory, circling around the city at night and destroying some of the boats by which the Pandis were still bringing troops into the city.

These adventures led to some fierce clashes and a number of Muzbees were killed. Their places were quickly taken by friends and relatives who had made their own way down to Delhi from the Punjab. In many cases they joined the ranks of the 'Punjab Sappers' under the names of men already killed in action. This simple expedient meant that they could immediately start to draw rations and it avoided delays with documentation. Duncan Home's sappers were a scratch force. In the heat of battle there was neither the time nor the inclination to create an elaborate administrative structure. The surviving records are therefore sketchy and unreliable, and it is difficult (if not impossible) to state exactly how many Muzbees served at Delhi, how many were killed and which individual men took part in the attack on the Kashmir Gate. These facts are a reflection of the speed and determination with which the siege was carried forward and the aggressive spirit of the men under Duncan's command.

There was plenty of fighting to be done, no lack of opportunity for any ardent young man anxious to prove himself and to win his spurs. The following letter was written to a friend by a 23-years-old artillery subaltern, James Hills, shortly after a typical excursion into the British lines by a party of mutineer cavalry:

> 'The alarm went, and off I started with my two guns to a position laid down for them, when, to my astonishment, through an opening on my right, only fifty yards off, dashed a body of cavalry. Now I tried to get my guns into action, but only got one unlimbered when they were upon me. I thought that by charging them I might make a commotion, and give the gun time to load; so in I went at the front rank, cut down the first fellow, slashed the next across the face as hard as I could, when two

sowars charged me. Both their horses crashed into mine at the same moment, and of course both horse and myself were sent flying. We went down at such a pace that I escaped the cuts made at me, one of them giving my jacket an awful slice just below the left arm – it only, however, cut the jacket. Well, I lay quite snug until all had passed over me, and then got up and looked about for my sword. I found it full ten yards off. I had hardly got hold of it when three fellows returned – two on horseback. The first I wounded, and dropt him from his horse; the second charged me with a lance – I put it aside, and caught him an awful gash on the head and face. I thought I had killed him; apparently he must have clung to his horse, for he disappeared. The wounded man then came up, but got his skull split. Then came on the third man – a young, active fellow. I found myself getting very weak from want of breath, the fall from my horse having pumped me considerably, and my cloak somehow or other had got tightly fixed round my throat, and was kindly choking me. I went, however, at the fellow, and cut him on the shoulder; but some "kapra" (cloth) on it apparently turned the blow. He managed to seize the hilt of my sword, and twisted it out of my hand; and then we had a hand-to-hand fight, I punching his head with my fists, and he trying to cut me, but I was too close to him. Somehow or other I fell, and then was the time, fortunately for me, that Tombs came up and shot the fellow. I was so choked by my cloak that move I could not until I got it loosened. By the by, I forgot to say that I fired at this chap twice, but the pistol snapped, and I was so enraged I drove it at the fellow's head, missing him, however. Then, when I got up, Tombs was so eager to get up to a mound near us, that I only picked up my sword and followed him. After being there some time, we came down again to look after the unlimbered gun which was left behind. When we got down I saw the very man Tombs had saved me from, moving off with my pistol (he had only been wounded, and shammed dead). I told Tombs, and we went at him. After a little slashing and guarding at both sides, I rushed in at him and thrust; he cleverly jumped aside and cut me on the head, knocking me down – not, however, stunning me, for I warded his next cut when down. Tombs, following him up, made him a pass, and up I jumped and had a slash at him, cutting him on the left wrist, nearly severing it. This made him turn round, and then Tombs ran him through. He very nearly knocked over Tombs, for he cut through his cap and pagrie, but, fortunately, did not even cut the skin. I fancy I am indebted again to Tombs for my life, for although I might have got up and fought, still I was bleeding like a pig, and, of course, would have had a bad chance. One thing, however, if Tombs had not been there the second time, I should have fought more carefully. It was the wish to polish off the fellow before Tombs could get up to him, that

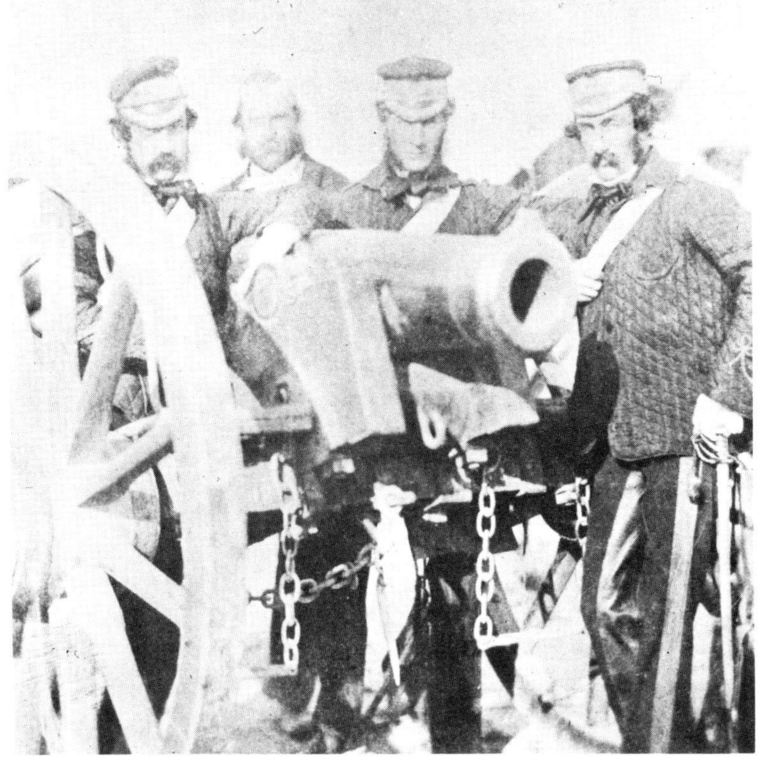

Officers of the Bengal Artillery photographed at Ferozepore in 1856. It was from this cantonment's arsenal that General Wilson received his siege train for the final assault on Delhi. The weapon pictured here is a 24-pounder muzzle-loading brass howitzer. The basic design of such pieces had changed hardly at all in the previous 150 years. Breech-loading and the rifled barrel were soon to revolutionise the deployment of field artillery. (India Office Library & Records)

made me rush at him in the way I did. I wanted awfully to bone the swords of the men I killed as trophies, but I was getting very faint, and had to come into my tent as fast as I could; but before I got the wound bound up the swords had been looted off. I lost an awful lot of blood, as two veins were cut through; but I fancy it did me good, keeping off inflammation. The wound was a beautiful one, just as if it had been done by a razor. It was four inches long, and down to the skull, a line being left on it; so I had a narrow escape. However, if I live to see the end of these mutinies, I shall have good reason to thank the "Sowars" for their charge, Tomb's name and mine having been sent up to the Governor-General by the Commander-in-Chief, the latter recommending us "worthy of the highest honour for distinguished bravery and gallantry".'

Both Hills and Tombs were subsequently awarded the Victoria Cross. Lieutenant Colonel Henry Tombs, the most senior officer to be so decorated for valour at Delhi, took overall command of the artillery during the siege. Initially he was hampered by the limited firepower of the Delhi Field Force, but Wilson's appeal for more guns, packing a bigger punch, was answered by the ordnance depôts still under British control.

On 4 September the last of the heavy guns arrived from Ferozepore. Wilson could expect no reinforcement from the south or east, his lines of communication being totally blocked by the Pandi forces in Cawnpore and Lucknow. His own forces were shrivelling away under the combined onslaught of heat, disease and enemy action, while the strength of his opponents had grown to 15,000 (and more mutineers were still coming across the Jumna from distant cantonments). It was a case of now or never. He told Baird Smith to start the final stage of preparation.

The plan of attack centred upon the construction of a number of new batteries, very close to the northern walls of the city. Once the heavy guns were in place, they would batter the principal bastions and attempt to

Lieutenant General Sir Archdale Wilson, Bengal Artillery (1803–1874). Apart from service at Bhurtpore in 1825–26 and some minor actions during the Punjab campaign of 1848–49, he had followed a relatively drab career. On 17 July, although still only a substantive Colonel, he took command of the Delhi Field Force. His predecessor (Reed) granted him the temporary rank of Brigadier General. Ten days later the Governor General confirmed the appointment and granted a further temporary promotion as Major General. After the battle he was confirmed in this rank, was made a Knight Commander of the Bath, was created a baronet as Sir Archdale Wilson of Delhi, and was granted an additional pension of £1,000 per annum 'for services at the siege of Delhi'. He received the thanks of the House of Commons, of the House of Lords, and of the Directors of the East India Company. In October 1857 he handed over command to Brigadier General Nicholas Penny and went to Mussoorie on sick leave. By February 1858 he was again fit for duty and took command of the Artillery Division at the recapture of Lucknow (and for his services there 'was publicly thanked in despatches by Sir Colin Campbell'). A few weeks later, on 10 April, he and his wife embarked for England in the P&O steamer 'Bengal' at Calcutta. Officially he was leaving India for three years' sick leave but, in the event, he never returned. In the space of a few months he had emerged from obscurity, commanded one of the most difficult operations of war ever undertaken by British forces, and then disappeared back into limbo. For a short while, greatness had been thrust upon him. Although lacking the temperament and the experience for such huge responsibilities, he achieved a very remarkable victory. (Engraving by D J Pound, National Portrait Gallery)

destroy the cannon mounted within them. Simultaneously they would hammer at selected points along the curtain walls between the bastions in order to make gaps through which the attacking infantry could force an entry into the city.

For the next seven days and nights the sappers laboured nonstop, under a heavy fire, to build emplacements for fifty-four guns and mortars. It was a scene of feverish activity, hundreds of men digging, building, and dragging forward sandbags and heavy timbers with the aid of bullocks and camels. Soon they were joined by the artillerymen who, each night, brought forward more heavy weapons. The most distant battery was 700 yards from its target, the closest only 140 yards! Their points of aim were the Moree Bastion to the right, the Kashmir Bastion in the centre, the Water Bastion to the left, and the twelve-feet-thick curtain wall between the latter two. Duncan Home personally supervised the construction of two of these batteries, including the closest, and worked under fire, day and night, all that week.

The ferocity of the city's defences, and the frantic speed with which the

The breaching of Delhi's walls would have been impossible without the heavy artillery ordered down to Delhi in August from Phillaur and Ferozepore. The van of the siege train reached the outskirts of Delhi on 3 September, reinforcing the lighter pieces despatched from Ferozepore on 16 May. The second (heavy) train consisted of six 24-pounders, eight 18-pounders, four 10-inch mortars, and four 8-inch mortars, all with 1,000 rounds of ammunition per piece. On the move, the convoy extended over thirteen miles of road and, each day, the head of the column was preparing to make fresh camp as the tail was starting to leave the previous resting ground! Throughout the siege, the arsenals at Phillaur and Ferozepore sent 2,000 cart-loads of ordnance down the Grand Trunk Road to Delhi. They supplied 80,000 rounds of shot and shell, 5,000 muskets, 500,000 pounds of powder and nearly 3,000,000 rounds of balled cartridge. (India Office Library & Records)

siege work was carried forward, were described by Lieutenant A M Lang, one of the few Bengal Engineer officers who found time to keep a diary. On 11 September he wrote:

> 'At 1 pm, I went with twelve Sappers and sixty Pioneers to No.2 Right to make the traverse and epaulments longer. The enfilade fire from the right-rear was dreadful; the gun-wheels, carriages, trails, platform ribands and traverses were struck again and again. Six Sappers and I on the parapet got lots of grape plugged at us; all missed, but men in the batteries were hit.'

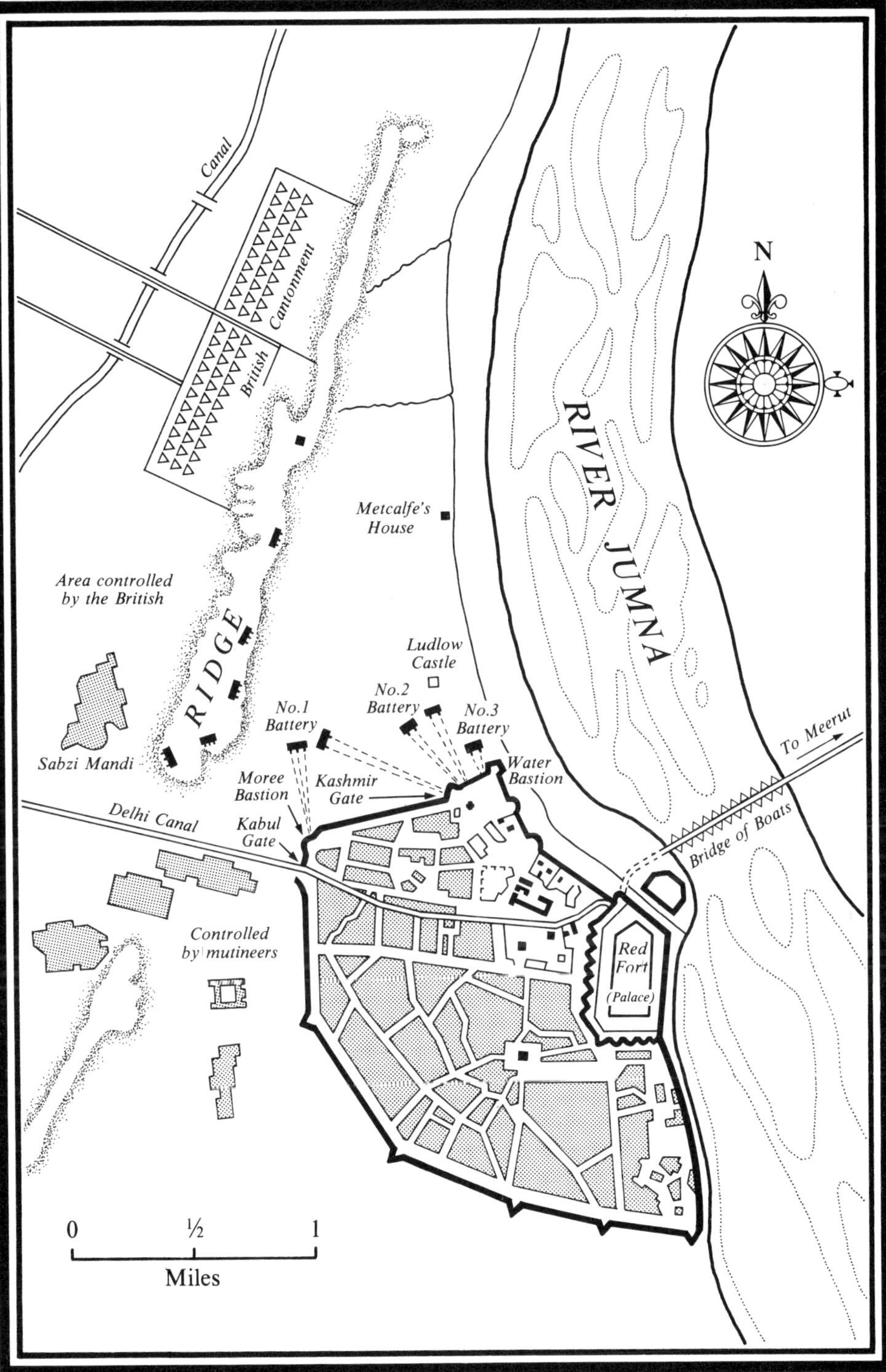

Canal
British
Cantonment
N
RIVER JUMNA
Metcalfe's House
Area controlled by the British
RIDGE
Ludlow Castle
No.2 Battery
No.1 Battery
No.3 Battery
Sabzi Mandi
Water Bastion
Moree Bastion
Kashmir Gate
To Meerut
Delhi Canal
Kabul Gate
Bridge of Boats
Controlled by mutineers
Red Fort
(Palace)
0
½
1
Miles

Captain (Brevet Lieutenant Colonel acting Brigadier General) John Nicholson, 1821–1857. This tall slender Irishman was only thirty-five at the time of his death. For sixteen years he had served almost continuously in the hills and mountains of Afghanistan and Kashmir, experiencing a series of adventures which would be unbelievable if they were not so well documented. His messianic personality had great influence upon the tribesmen, some of whom worshipped him as a demi-god. He played a key role in quelling the Mutiny in the Punjab before hurrying down to Delhi with a force of his fiercely loyal levies and irregular cavalry. He joined Wilson on the Ridge on 14 August and at once made forceful criticisms of the conduct of the siege. Certainly there was much with which to find fault, but Wilson was gradually settling the reins of command in his inexperienced hands. The crisis came a few days later when six thousand mutineers, with cannon and cavalry, sortied from the city and made a wide sweep around the British right flank to strike at their rear. Nicholson led the force which counter-attacked the Pandis and routed them at Najafgarh on 25 August. The line of communication was kept open, permitting the arrival of the heavy siege train and preparation for the final assault. Nicholson was nominated to lead the attack on Delhi in person. Shot through the body soon after scaling the walls, he lingered until 23 September and was then buried in the cemetery which bears his name. A truly heroic figure, John Nicholson would have undoubtedly risen to high rank had he lived. (Daguerrotype, National Army Museum)

His entry for 12 September was even more vivid:

> 'We are worked to the very limit of human power. As I come into my tent after a night out, my eyes are closing themselves and my senses quite foolish! I fling myself down with the sun up and am too tired to sleep but restlessly. Again, in excited dreams, I set parties to work under a hot fire, howl at them, urge them on, grape pouring in, and guns drowning one's voice. We are fighting close up now, hurrying on the most rapid of sieges, working recklessly under fire without approaches or parallels. Our big, smashing guns roar out together in salvoes and crash into the crumbling walls.'

As the batteries were completed so they came into action and pounded the selected targets. Beginning on 7 September, the gunners kept up a steady fire, gradually dismantling the opposing defences. They hammered the curtain wall, making two substantial breaches between the Kashmir and Water Bastions. Masonry was brought crashing down into the deep outer ditch where it formed a convenient bridge for assaulting infantry. The mutineers were still manning the walls and maintaining a heavy musketry and cannon fire at the besiegers (who were accepting heavy casualties throughout this period), but it was clear that the climax must come soon.

On the night of 13 September two reconaissance parties crept forward

to the very edge of the ditch (at the foot of the wall) to inspect the damage. One party consisted of Lieutenants Lang and Medley, the other was led by Duncan Home with Lieutenant Greathed. All four returned safely and reported that the breaches were indeed scaleable by infantry. Having heard their stories, Wilson decided to launch the assault that very morning (14 September). The full details of Wilson's plan of attack can be studied elsewhere but, in essence, he intended to launch approximately 5,000 men into the assault at first light. They were divided into five columns (the fifth being the reserve), each having approximately 1,000 bayonets, and each composed of British and Indian regiments in equal proportion. Overall command of the assault was given to Brigadier General John Nicholson.

The first column, led personally by Nicholson, would storm the breach near the Kashmir Bastion. The second column would make a similar rush at the breach near the Water Bastion. The third, commanded by Colonel George Campbell of the 52nd Regiment, would force its way directly through the Kashmir Gate (once it had been blown open). The fourth column would make a direct rush at the Lahore Gate. The fifth (and strongest) column would be thrown in to reinforce whichever of the first four columns was making the best progress. The artillery would fire over their heads as the columns advanced. During the final leg of the approach, the heavy guns would cease fire and skirmishers of the 60th Regiment (King's Royal Rifle Corps) – thrown forward of the columns – would try to make the defenders remain behind cover.

The plan was simple enough and could be readily understood by everyone taking part. It was equally evident to the enemy what Wilson intended to do. There could be no element of surprise in this dangerous venture. Wilson was committing almost his entire effective force to a head-on attack across open bullet-swept ground. If the assault failed it could not be repeated – he had no expectation of reinforcement. Desperate measures were needed to ensure that his troops could get inside the city quickly, and Wilson asked Baird Smith if one of his officers could lead a 'forlorn hope' against the key point, the Kashmir Gate. If a small group of men could go forward just before the assault was launched, and if they could blow in the heavy wooden doors with explosives, number three column would have a straight run into the city. The chances of success for the people taking part would be slim, the chances of survival even slimmer, but the attempt must be made.

Baird Smith consulted Captain Alexander Taylor and they selected Duncan Home as the man to command the 'explosion party'. He had just returned from his midnight inspection of the city walls and was familiar with the features of the ground to be covered. As an engineer he was experienced with explosives. As the senior available engineer lieutenant he was the obvious choice. So, with only a few hours to go, he swiftly organised his small group and made his plans.

His start-line was the ruined Ludlow Castle, approximately half a mile to the north of the Kashmir Gate and the site of one of the heavy siege batteries. Covered by a line of skirmishers provided by the 60th Regiment,

The Kashmir Gate photographed a few months after the battle. The bridge has been repaired, but in all other respects the scene is little changed from that which faced Duncan Home and his companions. The size of the large wooden doors blown open by the sappers can be judged from the human figure standing on the bridge. The right-hand portico, it should be noted, was sealed with brickwork at the time of the battle. (India Office Library & Records)

he intended to make his way toward the Gate, making use of what little cover remained on this shot-torn ground, and then sprint the final two hundred yards.

The party was split into two sections, each having a separate duty. Duncan would lead the first section (with three other men) and each man would carry a canvas bag of black powder weighing twenty-five pounds. The bags would be laid against the doors with fuses exposed for ignition. The second section, the 'firing party', led by Lieutenant Philip Salkeld of the Bengal Engineers, would come up immediately afterwards to ignite the fuses. This section (Salkeld and six other men) would be carrying a slow match and tamping bags (small sacks of sand to hold the explosives bags firmly against the doors).

Colonel Campbell's third column was late moving off from the Ludlow Castle position. The mutineers had been busy during the night, repairing the city walls and filling the breaches with sandbags. A final barrage by Wilson's artillery was needed to undo their work before his infantry could hope to force a way through. The sun was already over the horizon when the time came for Duncan to set his plan in motion. It would have been futile to blow the gates if the assault column had not been ready to rush in

immediately afterwards. Reaching the roadway leading to the Gate without loss, he paused for a moment for his stragglers to catch up and then gave the signal.

The party crossed the final stretch of open ground at the double, Duncan in the lead. His every move was watched anxiously by his general officer commanding, Archdale Wilson, who was perched 800 yards to the rear on the ruined walls of Ludlow Castle. Seated beside the general was Duncan's commanding officer, Baird Smith, who had struggled from his sick-bed to witness this historic moment. Baird Smith was ill with fever, had been shot through the ankle, and had some days earlier been shaken by a heavy fall from his horse, but he was determined to see his men in action. Duncan was probably not even aware of their presence, but rarely can a young officer have gone forward to almost certain death or injury in full view of such a high-ranking audience.

The objective consisted of an outer gateway, set in an earth bank, followed by a ditch twenty-five feet wide and ten feet deep. Beyond this was the main Kashmir Gate into which were set two large wooden casement door sections (one of them having a small wicket gate sufficient for one person at a time to enter). Between the outer gate and the main gate, there had been a substantial timber bridge crossing the ditch. When Duncan arrived, breathless with the exertion of carrying his share of the powder, he found the outer gate shattered by the earlier bombardments and hanging open. He charged through, onto the bridge, and dumped his bag at the foot of the main gate. He now discovered, however, that the bridge also had been damaged by cannon-fire and that the Pandis had removed much of the cross-planking. There was scant standing room on the remaining timbers for his small body of men to do their work.

He glanced around, saw Salkeld and some of his men racing forward through the outer gate, and jumped down into the ditch to make space for them. He was joined by Bugler Hawthorne of the 52nd Regt (Oxfordshire Light Infantry) who had arrived at the gate at the same time as his leader. So far everything had gone well. The marksmen on the high walls above them had been so amazed by the sight of this reckless handful of men running forward that they had momentarily ceased firing. Now, realising the intention of the attackers, they poured a torrent of small arms fire down onto the bridge. At ground level, more snipers opened the wicket gate and started to shoot straight across the bridge.

One of the first point-blank shots killed Sergeant Andrew Carmichael of the Bengal Sappers & Miners, one of Duncan's 'carrying party', as he was in the act of laying his charge. Another shot severely wounded Havildar Madho. The fourth 'carrier', Sergeant John Smith (also of the Bengal Sappers & Miners), laid his own and Carmichael's bags, calmly checked the position of the fuses and then stood to one side so that

Lieutenant Salkeld could apply the slow match.

At this point Salkeld was struck in the leg by a heavy musket ball. Another ball smashed his left arm. As he fell, and as he started to roll off the bridge into the ditch, the young officer held out the slow match to Sergeant Smith and told him to light the fuse. Instead, Corporal Burgess, one of Salkeld's own group, crouching near his stricken officer, reached out and took it. He saw instantly that it had in fact gone out and, shouting above the din of the musket fire, he asked Smith to pass him a box of matches. Then Burgess too was hit. He fell, sprawled across the bridge timbers, and would have fallen directly into the ditch if one of the Indian sappers had not held on to him. Bullets flew all about them, but the sapper successfully lowered the dying Corporal down to where Duncan and Bugler Hawthorne were crouching.

The shot-battered Kashmir Gate, photographed in 1977 but little changed from its condition in 1857. The outer ditch where Bugler Hawthorne sounded the 'advance' has been filled with hard-core, the old wooden bridge being replaced by a permanent causeway. The right-hand portico was walled-up at the time of the attack. Later, and for many years, the left portico was used by traffic leaving the city, the right by traffic entering. Today the Gate is little used. (Photograph by kind permission of Mrs J Harfield)

The implacable Sergeant Smith, now the only survivor still within reach of the explosives, knelt down by the doors, sheltering under the overhang of the gateway, and carefully struck a match. Instead of burning steadily, the fuse went off in his face and he knew that the main explosion was imminent. He hurled himself off the timberwork into the ditch. The stupefying blast of one hundred pounds of black powder hit him as he was still in mid-air; he arrived on the floor of the ditch in a deluge of smashed timber and broken brickwork. To his surprise he found himself uninjured, apart from a badly bruised leg. He joined Duncan Home and Bugler Hawthorne by the forward face of the ditch and they peered up through the smoke and dust to see what effect the explosion had had upon the doors. It was hard to judge just how much damage had in fact been done, but Duncan hesitated only a few seconds before ordering Bugler Hawthorne to sound the agreed 'success signal' – the regimental 'advance' of the 52nd Regiment.

Despite the dry dusty heat and his natural anxiety, Hawthorne managed to make a lip and sound the 'advance'. But the roar of the battle was now even louder and Duncan doubted whether the waiting Colonel Campbell could have heard the signal. Hawthorne stood in the centre of the floor of the ditch, musket balls tearing up the dust around his feet, and twice more he sounded. The urgent pealing call was smothered by the crackle of musketry and the heavy sullen roar of the city's guns.

One hundred yards to the rear, where Colonel Campbell and his adjutant were crouched behind a low stone wall, the signal was barely audible. Bugler Johnson, the colonel's orderly bugler that day, ran forward several yards and listened intently for the distinctive notes of his comrade's bugle. If anyone could detect the signal it was Johnson, his ear trained to accept pitch and tone. After a moment he heard Hawthorne's call, turned to his colonel and nodded, and Campbell waved his sword to signal the advance.

The advance storming party, headed by Captain J A Bailey, ran forward and, shouting and cheering with an almost hysterical excitement, went streaming over the shattered bridge. Packed in a tight single file, they raced through the gap where the right leaf of the double doors had been blown off its hinges. In later years, Bailey wrote his own account of the attack:

> '... about half-a-minute after the explosion we made a rush for the gate, the lower part of which was hidden from us by a rise in the ground. A few moments afterwards a bullet smashed my left arm just below the elbow joint and knocked me over; I was up at once, and hardly knew that I was wounded, but, during the slight delay caused by my endeavouring to pick up my sword and hat, my men had rushed past

14 September 1857: the first wave of the 52nd Regiment's storming party comes bursting through the Kashmir Gate. Led by Captain J A Bailey and Captain Charles Crosse, the leading company quickly occupied the area of the Main Guard and a section of the city wall. ('Illustrated London News' Picture Library)

me and were furiously crushing through the narrow opening in the glacis which was partly closed by a mantlet. The supports, which had come up while the powder was being laid, now joined the rear of the stormers, and closely followed by the Column, rushed headlong through the gate, most of the defenders of which had been killed or disabled by the explosion. They were all soon inside, but Crosse, who had run forward on seeing that I was wounded, was the first to enter.

The column, being speedily reformed, cleared the Cashmere and Water Bastions with the bayonet, and then set to work to fight their way through the narrow streets to the Jumma Musjid [*sic*] on the farther side of the town. Three other Columns, which had assaulted on our left, were now inside the walls, and the fifth, consisting of the picquets from the ridge and the Cashmere contingent, had orders to capture the battery at Kishengunge on the right and then join Nicholson ...'

More and more men followed on the heels of Captain Crosse and Captain Bailey. Later they joined with the other assaulting columns and, after nearly a week of bloody street fighting, the battle was won. But their success cost the attackers the fearful price of sixty-six officers and 1,104 other ranks killed and wounded, one third of their total strength.

Following hard on the heels of Colonel George Campbell's third column came the supporting units. One of these was a party of sappers under the command of Lieutenant George Chesney, Bengal Engineers. He saw that the shattered condition of the wooden bridge was preventing an adequate flow of reinforcements into the city. Rather than wait for new planks to be brought from the engineer field park, he told his men to lift the heavy door, blown flat by the force of the explosion, and to lay it across the main timbers as a new roadway. Within minutes Major Scott's field battery was clattering across the bridge and through the archway to join the embattled infantry. George Chesney (who later in life had a fine political career) was severely wounded while supervising these arrangements. However, his quick thinking turned what had been a major obstacle to the British assault into the means which ensured its success.

Down in the ditch the survivors took stock of their situation. At first dazed by the blast, they quickly realised that Carmichael and Burgess were beyond help but that Salkeld might still be saved. Sergeant Smith, with the help of Bugler Hawthorne, made the officer as comfortable as he could and then went off in search of medical aid. Duncan Home stayed with his friend for a while but, when he saw that Smith had the situation well in hand, he went forward through the shattered Kashmir Gate and later rejoined Colonel Campbell's third column.

He found the infantry locked in a savage battle of the most primitive kind; the mutineers defended every house and every narrow street with the desperation of men who knew that the most terrible retribution would fall upon them if they were captured. Hand-to-hand fighting gave limited opportunity for the skills of an engineer. Duncan found a sheltered corner and, ignoring the tumult of the battle, went to sleep. He had had little rest during the week preceding the assault and had not slept at all during the final thirty-six hours (when he was making his secret night reconnaissance of the defences).

A few hours later he was back in the fray and was almost immediately wounded. This did not prevent him from playing his part. On the following day, 16 September, he became even busier when ordered by Baird Smith to take over from Taylor as Field Engineer responsible for operations within the city. Taylor, although only thirty-one years of age, had worked himself to the point of exhaustion and, with many of his most experienced engineer officers now either dead, wounded or ill, he could no longer carry the full burden unaided.

Duncan was with the advancing troops during the following days of savage street fighting. Losses on both sides were severe and the assault

force commander, John Nicholson, had been badly wounded and was dying, but gradually the attackers fought their way towards the centre of the city and eventually reached the walls surrounding the Royal Palace. Most of the defenders fled, but a small group of fanatical mutineers remained inside. It seems likely that they had been smoking *bhang* and were half-drugged when the British reached the South Gate. Duncan Home ran forward with an explosive charge and blew in the doors. British troops followed on his heels and despatched the mutineers with the bayonet. This affair, at the scene of his Uncle's murder, must have given Duncan particular satisfaction.

By 20 September it was all over; the surviving mutineers streamed away across the Jumna and the capital city was once more in British hands. General Wilson's next task was to clear his lines of communication and to assist Sir Colin Campbell's veterans from the Crimean war in the recapture of Lucknow and Cawnpore. He split up his victorious force at Delhi, organised new columns, and sent them out to clear the surrounding area. One of these columns – consisting of 2,790 British and Indian troops under the command of Colonel Greathed of the 8th Regiment of Foot – was given the task of sweeping the Gangetic Doab (the area between the rivers Jumna and Ganges). It was a hot-bed of insurrection, many of the local civilians having joined with the mutineers in murdering the fleeing British refugees during the early stages of the rising. Duncan Home was attached to Greathed's column as Chief Field Engineer.

While it is true that large numbers of European men, women and children were murdered with great brutality by the mutineers, it is equally evident that some of the stories of torture, rape and bestiality were either grossly exaggerated or totally without foundation. Indeed, regarding the treatment of white women by their Pandi captors, it has not been possible to discover a single authenticated instance of sexual violation. However, the sentiment of the British relief forces was such that every Indian male capable of bearing arms was assumed, directly or by association, to be guilty of such crimes. Hundreds were killed in the days following the recapture of Delhi, either by shooting or by slow strangulation on improvised gallows. The latter punishment, which did not break the neck but simply asphyxiated the condemned man, was described with macabre accuracy as 'the Pandi hornpipe'. Thomas Cadell, who won his VC during the siege, wrote home to his sister: 'lots of blackguards are hanged every morning . . . the more the merrier . . . you say Delhi ought to be thoroughly destroyed . . . we say the same.' Cadell's wish almost came true; the city was looted, laid waste and its holy places desecrated, by the avenging victors.
(India Office Library & Records)

The column moved out of Delhi on 24 September, glad to leave behind the stinking streets still littered with bodies and the debris of battle. There is no doubt that the British troops were elated by the thought of bringing vengeance to anyone who, no matter how remotely, might have aided the mutineers. The Indians had sown the wind – now they would reap the whirlwind.

The line of advance took the column first to Secundrabad. Villages suspected of disloyalty were burned to the ground while others, where the terrified peasants were clearly innocent, were left in peace. By 28 September the force had reached the small city of Bolandshahr, still held in strength by rebel troops. After a sharp early morning battle – which left 300 Pandis dead in the streets – the British regained the city and made camp on the outskirts.

Patrols were sent out and onc of these inspected the deserted fort at Malagarh, five miles away. It was found to be packed with loot stolen by the mutineers from British homes and convoys. More importantly, the fort had been used until very recently as an arsenal. The Pandis had used it for the manufacture of weapons and explosives. Lacking professional supervision, and having abandoned it in a hurry, they had left large quantities of munitions scattered all over the place. The whole fort was a powder keg and a danger to anyone entering it. Duncan Home was given the job of dealing with these materials and blowing up the fortifications so that it could not be re-occupied by hostile forces after the British moved on.

For the next three days he worked with a small party of Bengal Sappers & Miners and some troopers from the 9th Lancers, sorting through the

The obverse of the elegant Mutiny medal awarded to 176,150 service personnel and civilians who served in the suppression of the rebellion. Designed by William Wyon RA, chief engraver to the Royal Mint, this 'young head' bust is found on many types of medal and coinage of the period. The medal was suspended by a distinctive red and white striped ribbon (which explains why the troops dubbed it 'the order of the blood and bandages').

The reverse of the Mutiny medal was designed by Leonard Charles Wyon (son of William). He succeeded to the post of chief engraver upon his father's death in 1851. The medal was issued without clasp, or with clasp(s) for 'Delhi', 'Defence of Lucknow', 'Lucknow', 'Relief of Lucknow' and 'Central India'. The rarest clasp is 'Defence of Lucknow', the second rarest is 'Delhi'. The majority of the medals originally awarded have been lost or melted down for scrap. (Photographs by Robert J Scarlett)

mounds of cartridges and barrels of powder. Sound material was carted away for use by the column, unstable munitions were stacked and systematically blown up by Duncan. His work was not entirely helped by the fact that the cavalrymen were unaccustomed to handling such dangerous ordnance. On the second morning he discovered two troopers sitting on a pile of powder kegs and cartridges, with loose powder scattered on the ground, happily smoking their pipes! His choice of language, when addressing these two, was well remembered in later years by a friend who witnessed the episode.

On the third and last day at Malagarh, with the pressures of the Delhi battle behind him and his work at the deserted fort almost completed, Duncan found time to compose a letter home to England:

'Camp, Malagarh,
near Bolundshuhur,
October 1st

My dear Mother,

In the hurry and work of the siege of Delhi the last mailday passed without my knowing it, or being able to write, and I am now on duty with the moveable column whose destination is not known and which has, as yet, only reached thus far, after an engagement with Walidad Khan's men at Bolundshuhur on Monday last. He bolted and has left the fort in our hands, which I am at present rendering untenable. You will doubtless, ere this, have heard of the fall of Delhi, and that the King is in our hands. Mogul Beg and two other princes [*sic*] have been killed. The former was the man who killed Uncle Simon. I must now tell you something about the siege, and of my goings on in it. For several days I was perpetually on duty, day and night, first on the right and then on the left. I had charge of the construction of our first breaching battery which was constructed in one night, a thing which has only been done in one other siege. The Engineers were highly complimented on it. I then had charge of the construction of the battery nearest the city – at only 140 yards from it – which was finished satisfactorily and breached the water-bastion of the city. I remained in charge of the battery till the assault, in which my duties were as follows: I was directed to take charge of a party of 14 Sappers, including three non-commissioned officers and another officer of Engineers named Salkeld, and ten privates, and blow in the Cashmere Gate of the city. Owing to delays the assault did not take place 'till sunrise, and I had to advance from Ludlow Castle (Uncle Simon's house) in broad daylight to the gate, place powder bags against it and explode them, and then give the signal for the advance. We all arrived at the gate quite safely, although we were under a very heavy fire of musketry from the walls and through the wicket of the gate, which was open. However, as we were laying the bags at the gate we began to lose men. There were two Engineer non-commissioned officers and one native killed. Salkeld was badly wounded in the arm and leg. He has lost his arm, and his leg being broken, is in splints. I hope he may recover, but it seems very doubtful. I had also two natives wounded. I myself escaped with a blow on the leg above the knee from a stone knocked up by a bullet. Out of 12 persons who were at the gate 6 were killed or wounded. For blowing in the Cashmere Gate, in broad daylight, General Wilson has put in orders that Salkeld, a sergeant, a bugler and myself are to get the Victoria

Cross, so we are, of course, properly proud, we being the first persons in the Indian Army [*sic*] to receive the decoration.

After we got into the city, owing to the heavy loss in Engineers, 9 out of 117 who went into action being killed or wounded, I was the third senior officer fit for duty, so got charge of the left column of attack, and was continually on duty until the King evacuated the Palace. I had never more than four hours' sleep in the 24 and then only by snatches.

I had also the pleasure of blowing in the gate of the Palace, though no one luckily fired at me, there being so few men left to guard the Palace, and they were asleep. The gate was blown in at noon. So now the Delhi business may be considered over, and I hope the country will soon begin to get settled.

We had a tolerably sharp action with the rebels at Bolundshuhur, which they took with about 2,000 men and some 14 guns. However, after three hours' fighting, they bolted. They had, however, managed to attack our baggage and to cut up two sick Europeans who were being carried in dhoolies. We found a lot of European property in the fort which had been looted from Bolundshuhur. Walidad Khan was some relation of the King of Delhi and had continually intercepted our communications during the row. He has now, I believe, gone to Rohilcund, which has been the refuge for the district. I do not know where we go to from this place. I believe that the force is to go to Agra, but I should not be astonished at its being ordered on to Cawnpore to join the force under Havelock.

It is quite cool in camp though the sun is still powerful. I have not received any letter from you by this mail but hope to get some soon.

With best love to all,
Believe me your affectionate son,
Duncan C. Home.'

Duncan sealed the letter and arranged for it to be taken, together with those of his companions, to headquarters at Bolandshahr (and ultimately to a place in the Home family archives). He then turned his thoughts back to the job in hand and his final task – the destruction of the fort's principal bastion. Quantities of powder had been buried under the foundations of this structure and everyone looked forward to seeing the spectacular effect of what should be a very satisfying bang.

Duncan cleared the area and made certain that everyone was under cover. What happened next is best described by his friend and assistant, Lieutenant Arthur Lang of the Bengal Engineers, who wrote an account to Duncan's brother (Lieutenant Robert Home, of the same Corps):

'For the last three days we have lived in the Fort, blowing up and destroying its defences; your brother was so very happy about it,

Lieutenant Duncan Home VC, the man whose resource and courage ensured the success of the Kashmir Gate attack, whose name was stamped instantly upon the pages of India's history, and whose life was to end so violently only three weeks later. An impression drawn by Kenneth Petrie; he also made the sketch of Bugler Hawthorne in action, page 29.

enjoying so much each explosion, and considering it great amusement. Five mines yesterday and to-day he had with his own hands exploded, and one important one alone remained to blow in the counterscarp and thus connect the exterior and interior of the Fort. He laughed as he called to us all to clear away, and cried to the sergeant, "Now we will blow this one up and march off all jolly to camp."

The only two other officers here, Stevenson of the 23rd and I, ran up to the ruins of a bastion near, and I saw him run up to the slow-match with his port-fire in his hand. Heaven only knows how, but instantaneously the mine sprung, to our horror! We rushed down and called all the men to dig, but after a moment I looked round to see if I could see him anywhere near, and in a hollow some fifteen yards off I found your poor brother's body. He must have been killed instantly; life was extinct, and under the dreadful circumstances luckily so, for his legs were both broken, one in two places, and his arm was nearly torn off. He was a favourite with all in camp, brave and active, so very good-natured and always laughing. I am sure every one will mourn his loss, as I do, most deeply. Poor fellow! fancy escaping untouched from the blowing in of the Cashmere Gate, where he and Salkeld earned the Victoria Cross, to meet his end in exploding mines before a deserted fort. It is not now half an hour since the accident occurred.'

Duncan's body was taken to Bolandshahr for burial. He rests there to this day. The epitaph on his tomb unemotionally states his acheivement:

'In memory of Lieutenant Duncan Charles Home, Bengal Engineers, aged 29, who was killed by the explosion of a mine when engaged in destroying the Fort of Melagarh on the 1st October 1857. As leader of the "Forlorn Hope" which on the 21st September 1857 successfully attacked the Cashmere Gate, Delhi, he was awarded the first Victoria Cross given in India.'

The inscription is inaccurate; the Kashmir Gate was blown on 14 September and his was not the first Victoria Cross. But these minor errors cannot detract from the memory of an exceptionally brave and enterprising young Englishman. His story, and the glory won by his companions, was commemorated two decades later when a tablet was mounted on the shot-riddled ruins of the Kashmir Gate:

'On the 14th of September 1857, the British Force stormed Delhi. It was after sunrise on that day that the party, advancing from Ludlow Castle in the face of heavy fire, and crossing this bridge which had been totally destroyed, lodged powder bags against and blew in the right leaf of these gates, thus opening the way for the assaulting columns. This memorial is placed here as a tribute of respect to those gallant soldiers by General Lord Napier of Magdala, Colonel R.E. and C.-in-C. in India, 1876.'

The inscription on the tablet lists a roll of honour of officers and men who succeeded in reaching the bridge:

Bengal Engineers	– Lieutenant Duncan Home Lieutenant Philip Salkeld (mortally wounded)
Bengal Sappers & Miners	– Sergeant John Smith Sergeant A B Carmichael (killed) Corporal F Burgess (killed) Subadar Toola Ram Jemadar Bis Ram Havildar Madho (wounded) Havildar Tilok Singh (mortally wounded) Sepoy Ram Heth (killed)
52nd Foot	– Bugler Robert Hawthorne

Four of these men (Home, Salkeld, Smith and Hawthorne) were awarded the highest form of recognition for valour which a British monarch may bestow – the Victoria Cross.

APPENDIX A

The Victoria Cross

In 1854, almost exactly forty years after Waterloo, Great Britain found herself once again involved in a major war. Four decades of relative peace were shattered when she allied herself with France and Turkey in conflict with Russia. The Crimea campaign became notorious for the inadequacies of the British military establishment: uniforms, weapons, communications, medical facilities, generalship, all were found to be sadly lacking when placed under the strain of battle. But the same campaign revealed the fact that British soldiers had not lost the courage and endurance of their forebears in Wellington's 'army of the Peninsula'. The opening battles of the campaign were illuminated by many acts of outstanding individual heroism and it was these which brought to a head the debate regarding medallic honours and awards. The Distinguished Conduct Medal was introduced (for the army), also the Conspicuous Gallantry Medal (for the navy), but these were available only for other ranks and did not necessarily apply to specific instances of exceptional courage. There was need for a new award, one which could be bestowed upon officers and other ranks alike, naval and military.

After detailed discussion and correspondence (primarily between the War Office, the government, Queen Victoria and Prince Albert), agreement was reached. The award would be known as the Victoria Cross, it would be open to all ranks in the armed forces, it would be confirmed solely and entirely at the discretion of the Queen herself, and it would be the highest form of reward for valour in the face of the enemy. The Warrant, setting out precise details of eligibility and issue, was signed by the Queen on Tuesday, 29 January 1856. Thirteen months later, on 24 February 1857, *The London Gazette* carried the names of the first recipients. On 26 June of the same year, in Hyde Park, the Queen presented sixty-two of the 111 Crimea VC recipients with their medals. From that day onwards the VC was (and still is) recognised as the supreme honour to which any British or Commonwealth serviceman can aspire.

While Queen Victoria was engaged in rewarding her sailors and soldiers for their services in the Crimea, more soldiers were shedding their blood in another distant conflict, the suppression of the Great Sepoy Mutiny. The violence of that event was distinguished, just as the Crimea campaign had been, by many acts of great bravery. By the time the rebellion had run its course, the award of 182 Victoria Crosses had been recommended. Four of these were awarded to men who had taken part in the 'desperate task' at the Kashmir Gate. Two of them – Home and Salkeld – did not live to see their small crosses of bronze, and their premature deaths created a unique problem for the authorities.

The original VC Warrant made no provision for posthumous awards. When the possibility of an award for a deceased soldier first arose, the Secretary of State for War, Lord Panmure, gave his own ruling: '. . . this decoration will not be conferred upon the families of deceased officers . . . it is more in the nature of an order like that of the Bath than of a Medal in commemoration of a campaign or expedition . . . it is by survivors only that claims to the VC will be able to be established.' This ruling in fact held good for the next forty-six years. But the circumstances attaching to Home and Salkeld were unprecedented. They had been told by the General Officer Commanding, immediately after the battle, that they would receive the Victoria Cross. Major General Wilson was familiar with the terms of the Warrant and he knew that he was empowered, under Rule 7, to make such a decision. The relevant ruling stated:

> 'It is ordained that the Decoration may be conferred on the spot where the act to be rewarded by the grant of such Decoration has been performed under the following circumstances:
> I. When the Fleet or Army in which such an act has been performed, is under the eye and command of an Admiral or General Officer commanding the forces.
> II. Where the naval or military force is under the eye and command of an Admiral or Commodore commanding a squadron or detached naval force, or of a General commanding a Corps, or division or brigade, on a distinct and detached service, when such Admiral, Commodore or General Officer shall have the power of conferring the Decoration on the spot, subject to confirmation by Us.'

It was under the terms of the second part of this rule that Wilson conferred the VC upon Duncan Home and Philip Salkeld, and upon Sergeant Smith and Bugler Hawthorne. In the case of the latter two there was no difficulty: they both survived the campaign and received their medals in person. The two officers, however, died between the time that Wilson made his announcement in India and the date when the awards could be approved by the Queen and published in *The London Gazette*.

'For valour' – one of the Victoria Crosses awarded in 1858. The title of the award is far more than a dutiful courtesy to the then monarch. Queen Victoria and her husband took a deep interest in the evolution and detailed design of the Cross, and it was she who decided that it should be struck in bronze. Her criticisms and suggestions – of a surprisingly technical nature – referred to the prototype made in the workshops of Hancock & Company, jewellers, of London. One of their engravers, Mr H H Armstead, was the craftsman to whom the original design is attributed. Hancocks are the sole manufacturers of the VC and they still use bronze held in ingot form at the Central Ordnance Depôt, Donnington. The ingot was made from Russian cannon captured in the Crimea. For many years two different ribbons were used: dark red for military recipients, dark blue for naval personnel. A new Warrant in 1918 stated that dark red should be the standard colour for VC awards to all recipients, regardless of service or branch. (Photograph by Robert J Scarlett)

At first glance the anomalies in the terms of the Warrant made it seem that the medals could not be issued, even though the Queen might give her consent and approval to Wilson's Order. However, after little discussion, it was decided that Lord Panmure's earlier ruling did not apply in the cases of Home and Salkeld (and of three other men who similarly had died before the GOC's awards could be gazetted). As Sir Edward Lugard explained in a memorandum to the Military Secretary at the Horse Guards in January 1861: 'in cases in which the Cross has been provisionally conferred at the time, but the officer or soldier has died prior to the confirmation of the grant by Her Majesty, the Cross has, by Her Majesty's command, been forwarded to the legal representative, or nearest relative, with the expression of the satisfaction which it would have afforded Her Majesty to confirm the grant, had such officer or soldier survived.'

Duncan Home's VC was sent to his father, Major General Richard Home, with a suitably worded covering letter (as described by Sir Edward Lugard) dated 7 July 1858. On the same day the War Office despatched Philip Salkeld's VC to his father, the Reverend Robert Salkeld.

Thus the problem in this instance was solved, but the whole question of posthumous awards and claims by relatives remained a bone of contention for many years afterwards. Such claims referred not only to the Mutiny but also to other campaigns and wars fought by Queen Victoria's armies. All were steadfastly refused by the authorities, the argument being that the VC could be awarded only to surviving participants. It was not until January 1907 that the persistence of a few next-of-kin so moved 'the ultimate fount of honour' – King Edward VII – that there was a change of heart. The King approved the retroactive issue of six Crosses to the relatives of men whose actions were judged to have been particularly worthy of recognition. No amendment was made to the terms of the Royal Warrant, but a precedent was created and it was this change in the accepted qualifying procedures which formed the basis for all the posthumous awards made during the Great War of 1914–18. Not until 1920 did the authorities finally reach the decision to amend the Warrant formally, thereby giving full recognition to the concept of posthumous reward.

It is interesting to find the names of Home and Salkeld frequently cited in the correspondence which flowed between the War Office and the King prior to his *volte face* late in 1906. The two young Bengal Engineer officers had become not only part of the history of the Indian Mutiny but also, coincidentally, part of the history of the Victoria Cross itself.

There was one other anomaly attaching to these awards which is of interest. Strictly speaking, Home, Salkeld and Smith were not eligible for the Victoria Cross. They were in the service of the army of the Honourable East India Company, a 'private army' which had an establishment quite separate from that of the British Army. The terms of the original Warrant of 29 January 1856, drawn up at a time when every eye in Great Britain was turned in the direction of the Crimea, stated in its preamble that the new award should be 'highly prized and eagerly sought after by the officers and men of Her Majesty's Naval and Military forces.' Evidently the people who drafted the Warrant had in mind nothing more than services rendered by *Crown* forces.

The outbreak of the Mutiny in India soon revealed the deficiency in the terms of the Warrant. It is true that Clause 12 ('It is ordained that cases may arise not falling within the rules above specified . . . We will . . . confer the decoration . . .') provided a degree of flexibility, but Lord Panmure had an exasperating preoccupation with legal definitions, and he took the view that an amending Warrant was required. This was duly drawn up and was signed by the Queen on 29 October 1857 (by which time Home and Salkeld were already dead). In any event, a copy of this new Warrant (which made no reference to retroactive awards) did not reach India until early in 1858, by which time dozens of names had been recommended.

The officers of the East India Company were thrown into some confusion when they realised, for the first time, that the original Warrant did not technically permit them to nominate their own men. Confusion was worse compounded when it was pointed out that native troops serving with John Company regiments were already eligible (and had been since 1837) for their own equivalent of the Victoria Cross – the Indian Order of Merit.

After much debate it was agreed that acts of valour by *European* officers and men in the employ of John Company would be rewarded with the VC, even for those acts which pre-dated the signing of the amending Warrant of 29 October 1857. In the case of *Indian* troops, however, outstanding valour would continue to be recognised by the award of the Indian Order of Merit.

At first glance, the exclusion of Indians from eligibility might be thought symptomatic of racial prejudice. As a later appendix makes plain, this was not the case. However, it is a fact that fifty-four years were to pass before eligibility was extended to include non-Europeans serving with the Indian Army. On 21 October 1911, three weeks before sailing for India to attend the Delhi Durbar, King George V signed a new amending Warrant.

Full parity had at long last been achieved, irrespective of race, creed or colour. It is ironic that the decision came when it did. Only three years later, in the closing months of 1914, Indian troops found themselves thousands of miles from their native hills and plains, fighting in the mud of Flanders and winning some of the earliest Victoria Crosses of the great European war.

In recent decades it has been observed that the criteria needing to be satisfied, before a VC recommendation can be approved, have become markedly more stringent, perhaps too much so. Even during the war of 1914–18, it was the opinion of many soldiers that 'the VC is only given to dead men'. This apparently cynical view is supported, at least in part, by the known facts.

The statistics provide unlimited scope for those who may wish to debate the relative merit of VCs won in this battle or that, by one regiment or another, in an earlier decade or a later. Certainly there is some justification to the view that the standards pertaining during the war of 1939–45 were so demanding that the small cross of bronze must have seemed unattainable to the fighting men for whom it was intended. There is always the danger that any form of reward which is placed too high above the possible reach of those who seek it may, with time, cease to attract their interest. We should remind ourselves of the carefully chosen words of Queen Victoria's original preamble to the Warrant: '... the purpose (of the decoration) is that of rewarding individual instances of merit and valour ... We have instituted and created ... a new Naval and Military Decoration, which We are desirous should be highly prized and eagerly sought after by the Officers and Men of Our Naval and Military Services ...'.

The essential purpose of the VC is illuminated by the key words '...

The opening months of the Great War witnessed some outstanding acts of bravery and self-sacrifice. The British Expeditionary Force was fighting for its very existence. The Indian Corps came to the aid of the British and played a key role in preventing the Germans from breaking through to the Channel ports. The Corps included battalions from many parts of India and Nepal. One such was the 4th Bn Duke of Connaught's Tenth Baluch Regiment, and one of their men was Sepoy Khudadad Khan. A machine-gunner, he fought in the first battle of Ypres. On 31 October 1914, despite a desperate resistance, his section was swamped by massed grey ranks of German infantry near Hollebeke (Belgium). Every single man was shot or bayoneted to death, only Khudadad surviving. Severely wounded, he was left for dead on the battlefield but, hours later, he crawled back to rejoin his regiment. His award of the Victoria Cross was the first ever made to an Indian. (National Army Museum)

highly prized and eagerly sought after . . .', an objective which was achieved fully at Delhi by the readiness of the senior officers to acknowledge the many acts of heroism by the men under their command. The function and value of the award was further enhanced by the swiftness with which it could be granted. In an age when communications were inevitably slow and unreliable, there was great merit in the terms of Rule 7 which empowered a General Officer Commanding to make what was, in effect, an 'immediate' award. Not only did it reward the individual for his very recent act of valour, it also inspired his comrades and gave cause that they might seek to emulate his courage in the next phase of that same battle or campaign.

The inherent weakness of Rule 7 was the risk that one GOC might prove to be more or less generous than another in his interpretation of 'valour'. Clearly, the esteem in which it is held would have been undermined if the Cross had, at any stage, been too easily achieved. The Indian Mutiny was therefore the last campaign in which Rule 7 was exercised and it later disappeared from the terms of the Royal Warrant.

Since 1920, when provision for posthumous awards was belatedly incorporated in the wording of the Royal Warrant, fully 50.0% of VC recipients have not been able to receive their decorations in person because they were killed during the action which led to their recommendation, or they died of wounds shortly thereafter. This sad statistic is true not only of the world war of 1939–45, but also of the Korean and Vietnam wars. The ultimate exercise of the 1920 Warrant was seen in the wake of the battle for the Falkland Islands in 1982. Six men were recommended for the VC, only two were approved and they were both posthumous awards.

Quite apart from the statistics relating to living and dead recipients, it is instructive also to consider the total numbers of Crosses resulting from specific campaigns and comparing them with the proportionate numbers

of soldiers and sailors engaged in those campaigns. There were no more than 5,000 Europeans in the Delhi Field Force and yet they received 43 Victoria Crosses. By comparison, only four VCs were awarded for the battle of Arnhem, one of the bitterest contests of all time. The landings in Normandy, on 6 June 1944, resulted in just one such award. At first glance, it might seem that the large numbers of Crosses received by the men who fought in the Crimea and during the Mutiny are somehow less meritorious or less demanding of our respect. Many would argue that this is certainly not so, but that the authorities appear now to have become reluctant to exercise the powers vested in them by virtue of Queen Victoria's original wish.

By the same token, it might be said that the honorific value of the Cross was diminished when it was awarded to each and every qualifying participant in a particular action. Such a suggestion, were it made, could be swiftly refuted. The paucity of recognition by authority in the mid-twentieth century need not imply a diminution in the status of the Delhi awards. There have been other occasions when great bravery has been recognised by a multiplicity of awards.

Amongst a long list of comparable battles we find: the Alma, 1854 (8 VC awards); Inkerman, 1854 (24); Taku Forts, 1860 (7); the Andamans, 1867 (5); Rorke's Drift, 1879 (11); Omdurman, 1898 (4); Elandslaagte, 1899 (4); Sanna's Post, 1900 (5); Neuve Chapelle, 1915 (12); Gallipoli, 25–26 April 1915 (15); Gallipoli, 7–9 August 1915 (10); the first day of the Somme, 1916 (10); Zeebrugge, 1918 (8); and Peronne, 1918 (7, of whom 6 were Australians).

Full details of the VCs awarded for services at Delhi appear in Appendix J of this volume. While reading those citations, it is well to remember that the acts of valour which they describe were performed by men who had been marching and fighting for many weeks previously, who were already debilitated by chronic dysentery and heat exhaustion, and who found themselves part of a very small force isolated in a hostile land. Many were already at the end of their tether when they grimly fixed bayonets and went forward to the final assault.

Finally, and to illuminate the perils of comparing one award with another, there is the fact that only seventeen Distinguished Conduct Medals were approved for services by British troops at Delhi. It could be argued that, with nearly three times as many VCs awarded, the DCM was the harder to win. Perhaps the paradox proves – if proof be called for – that the piece of bronze or silver is less important than the quality of the man who once wore it upon his breast.

APPENDIX B

The (Indian) Order of Merit

In 1834 the Governor General of India submitted his proposal to the Court of Directors of the Honourable East India Company that two military orders should be sanctioned for the native troops and native officers of the Company's armies. One would be a reward to commissioned officers only, it would be a recognition of 'long, faithful and honourable service', and it would be known as the Order of British India. The other would be open to all ranks irrespective of seniority and service, it would be a recognition of 'conspicuous gallantry in the field', and it would be known as the Order of Merit.

The Governor General supported his recommendation with a list of reasons to justify the innovation. Not least of his arguments was that which exposed the inequality between commissioned officers of the two races: British officers serving in India were eligible for the Order of the Bath, Indian officers were not. Another argument pinpointed the unfairness of a system which permitted a British officer to be rewarded for gallantry in the field, but made no provision for the sepoys and sowars who had shown equal (or even greater) bravery in the face of the enemy.

The Directors considered the matter for nearly three years before accepting the proposal.

The introduction of the OBI (see Appendix C) came only a few years after the introduction of Long Service & Good Conduct medals for soldiers and sailors of the Crown forces and, although the OBI was intended exclusively for officers while the LS&GC medals went exclusively to non-commissioned officers, other ranks, petty officers and ratings, at least there is some parallel in the manner in which both Delhi and London were attempting, each in their own way, to reward long and faithful service.

The story of the IOM, on the other hand, is interesting in that Delhi was nearly twenty years ahead of London. As we have already seen, the common soldiers and sailors serving Queen Victoria went unrewarded until the Crimean campaign ushered in the DCM, the CGM and the VC.

The (Indian) Order of Merit of the 1837–1912 type. The star of the First Class was made entirely of gold, that of the Second Class was of silver but with gold laurel wreath surround, and the Third Class was entirely of silver. The badge was worn upon the left breast, suspended from a broad ribbon of dark blue with red edges. Only forty members of the Order ever achieved the distinction of the First Class, and only one hundred and thirty the Second Class. (Photograph by Robert J Scarlett)

To this extent the soldiers of John Company were better placed than their British counter-parts. In parenthesis, the Order of Merit instituted in India in 1837 is not connected in any way with the identically-named honour established in 1902 by King Edward VII. This class of honour, limited to a membership of twenty-four British persons at any one time, is intended to give 'special distinction in recognition of eminent services rendered by men and women in the arts of war, literature, science and other specialised fields'.

The preamble to the rules governing the award of the (Indian) Order of Merit stated:

> 'The object of this institution is to afford personal reward for personal bravery without reference to any claims founded on mere length of service and general good conduct. The Order is to consist of three classes, the two junior to be distinguished by a badge of silver, and the senior by a badge of gold, in the shape of a military laurelled star, bearing in its centre the inscription "The Reward of Valour". This badge is to be worn on the left breast, pendant from a dark blue ribbon with red edge.'

The rules then set out the terms under which the three different classes of the Order might be awarded.

> 'Third class: is to be obtained by any conspicuous act of individual gallantry on the part of any native officer or soldier in the field or in the attack or defence of fortified places, without distinction of rank or grade.

Second class: is to be obtained by those who already possess the third (class), and for similar services.

First class: is to be obtained, in like manner, only by those who already possess the third and second classes.'

The rules went on to specify the procedures for recommendation to the Order, making it clear that the Governor General alone was competent to confer admission. The final clauses must have attracted considerable interest within the ranks of the fighting regiments:

'Admission into the Order of Merit will confer on a member an additional allowance, equal in the third class to one third, in the second class to two-thirds, and in the first to the entire of the ordinary pay of his rank, over and above that pay or the pension he may be entitled to on retirement.

The widow of a member will be entitled to receive the pension conferred by the Order upon her husband, for three years after the date of his decease; and in the case of a plurality of wives, the first married is to have the preference.'

Apart from the honour bestowed by the award, the new decoration was clearly intended to have tangible value for the native troops and their families. Indeed, when in 1856 the Victoria Cross was introduced, with its additional pay for recipients of £10.00 per annum, it became evident that the OM in some cases carried a higher financial reward than the unfamiliar bronze cross. It is not known to what extent the regiments were consulted in the matter, but Lord Canning made it clear (when the possibility of awarding the VC to native troops was being aired in 1857) that he wished the OM to continue to be the supreme award for Indians.

It is against this background that we must view the distribution of honours and awards at the conclusion of the assault on Delhi. General Wilson had personally observed the advance of Duncan Home and his party and had decided on the spot to award the VC to the four Europeans who were still alive at the end of the day. He could not make the same gesture in the case of Sergeant Carmichael and Corporal Burgess, because Clause 7 of the VC Warrant made no provision for posthumous awards (not in the sense in which such awards later came to be known). Similarly, he could not award the VC to the natives of the Bengal Sappers & Miners (even if he had so wished) because such a thing had never been contemplated. However, it was evident that the Indians had shown courage of the highest quality, certainly courage of the kind which would have earned some of them a VC award if their skin had been white rather than brown, so Wilson ordered his staff to prepare a list of men worthy of admission to the Order of Merit.

It is at this point that the historian encounters a minefield of difficulties. Several lists have appeared in print over the years, each purporting to be an accurate roll of the Indian officers and sappers of Duncan Home's select band. None of the rolls agree one with another. Some discrepancies are to be expected, of course, because the first roll was prepared by a harassed aide on Wilson's staff at the end of a long and exhausting battle, because the party was a scratch force (soon dispersed) consisting of people who did not all know each other, and because the anglicised spelling of Indian names is subject to vagaries of fashion and personal taste. But these are the least of one's problems in ascertaining the truth.

One account states that Duncan was accompanied by 'fourteen native sappers'. Another source tells us that he had 'fourteen Bengal Sappers & Miners and ten Punjab Pioneers'. Yet another author quotes a total of thirty-three sappers, a number which clearly could not have been possible in such a confined space. Duncan Home, in his post-battle report, names four Indians only as having played an active or meritorious part. This number is confirmed (for survivors only) on Lord Napier's commemorative plaque of 1876, but the names themselves are not the same in each case!

The present author has adopted a solution to the dilemma which he judges to be incontrovertible. The following is a verbatim extract from the Governor General's Order No 579 of 1858, published in Allahabad on 15 December 1858:

> 'The Right Honourable the Governor General is pleased to confer the following rewards on the undermentioned Native officers and men of the Corps of Sappers & Miners, in special recognition of the conspicuous gallantry displayed by them in the demolition of the Cashmere Gate of the Fort of Delhi, on the 14th September 1857, as well as their good service and gallantry on other occasions:

Subadar Toola	To be a Member of the 1st class of the Order of Merit, and of the 2nd class of the Order of British India, with the title of Bahadoor
Jemadar Ramteroz Jemadar Bisram	To be Subadars, and Members of the 2nd class of the Order of Merit, and of the 2nd class of the Order of British India with the title respectively of Bahadoor
Jemadar Hunnoman Sing	To be Subadar, and a Member of the 2nd class of the Order of Merit, as Subadar

Havildar Adjoodhya Pattuk Havildar Hurpal Sing Havildar Bisnath Sing	To be Members of the 3rd class of the Order of Merit
Havildar Nunda Havildar Hurbuns	To be Jemadars, and Members of the 3rd class of the Order of Merit
Naick Sheikh Abdool Naick Nehal Khan Naick Devideen Naick Ungnoo	To be Members of the 3rd class of the Order of Merit
Sepoy Thakoordeen Sepoy Tewarry Sepoy Ramsooful Sepoy Opudhya	To be Members of the 3rd class of the Order of Merit'

It will be seen that seventeen men were honoured (four officers, nine non-commissioned officers, and four private soldiers). It is frustrating to find that only one of these men is mentioned in Duncan Home's post-battle report to Baird Smith (*vide* Appendix D). The Subadar Tooloo Ram mentioned by Duncan is clearly the Subadar Toola who headed the Governor General's list, but none of the other three names mentioned by Duncan resemble even remotely those subsequently honoured. Similarly, John Smith's account (*vide* Appendix G) does not help us because he mentions only one Indian, Havildar Tillok Singh (also mentioned by Duncan), but he died of his wound before he could be honoured. Lord Napier's plaque shows the names of Toola Ram and Jemadar Bis Ram, over whom there is no dispute, and it also mentions Havildar Madho, whom Duncan commended in his report, but who does not appear in the Governor General's honours list.

It is probable that several of the Indians had more than one name (in the same way that a European has a family name and various Christian names), and that they were known to their comrades and on their documents in more than one style or manner. It is also probable that Duncan was unable to establish the exact details of the junior ranks prior to composing his report; it was written in the closing stages of a furious week-long battle and his little party had by then been scattered over a wide area in and around the city. It was only with time and the return of calm that further investigations could be made by the staff who, with the benefit of access to muster rolls, could attempt to establish the precise facts. It will be noted that the Governor General's list emerged in December 1858, fourteen months after the event.

In 1932 the Commandant, KGO Bengal Sappers & Miners, authorised the publication of a 'correct list' of men who had represented the Corps at

the Kashmir Gate. There are thirteen names on this list, eight of whom appear on the Governor General's list and one of whom was a known casualty. Presumably the Commandant's staff had access to Corps documents and service records, hence this list has a ring of authenticity. However, at the end of the day, some discrepancies remain and we are left with a quandary.

Bearing in mind that all recommendations for the award of the OM needed to pass through a long and rigorous process of examination before reaching the Governor General's desk, the author prefers to assume that the only reliable list is that published by his office in 1858. It is clear that not all of these men actually passed through the outer gate and stood on

Representatives of each of the Indian regiments which fought at Delhi under General Wilson's orders are depicted here at John Nicholson's memorial. This belated recognition of the vital part played by loyal sepoys and sowars was published in 1911. The uniforms – and the titles of the regiments – had changed in the intervening fifty-four years, but the units illustrated are (from left of right): 1st King George's Own Sappers & Miners, 21st Prince Albert Victor's Own Cavalry (Frontier Force) (Daly's Horse), 57th Wilde's Rifles (Frontier Force), 22nd Sam Browne's Cavalry (Frontier Force), 3rd Queen Alexandra's Own Gurkha Rifles, 55th Cole's Rifles (Frontier Force), 2nd King Edward's Own Gurkha Rifles (The Sirmoor Rifles), and continuing with the man in the background holding a lance, 9th Hodson's Horse, 10th Duke of Cambridge's Own Lancers (Hodson's Horse), 32nd Sikh Pioneers, Queen's Own Corps of Guides, 54th Sikhs (Frontier Force), and 127 Queen Mary's Own Baluch Light Infantry. (Watercolour by Major A C Lovett, 'The Armies of India' by MacMunn)

the shattered bridge leading to the Gate. There was insufficient space there. But the honoured men undoubtedly all played an important part in the overall success of the operation and, if they had been British, some would have received the Victoria Cross. Further, we may accept Subadar Toola (Tooloo Ram), Havildar Madho (Madhoo), Havildar Tillok (Tilluk Singh) and Sepoy Jahub Singh (Sahib Singh) as having particularly distinguished themselves (even though Subadar Toola is the only one of this quartet to appear in the Governor General's list in readily identifiable form).

One of the most remarkable men included in the list was Jemadar Hunnoman Sing. As a young sapper, he had been wounded in the battle of Bhurtpore in 1825, thirty-two years earlier! Later he had fought in the disastrous First Afghan war and was one of the twenty-three sappers who were besieged in the fort at Kalat-i-Ghilzai in 1842. Later still he fought with distinction in the Sikh wars and was admitted to the OM in the 3rd class.

The importance attaching to the blowing of the Kashmir Gate is reflected in the scale of honours and awards to the participants. This was particularly so in the case of the four Indian officers. Subadar Toola, whose rank was equivalent to that of lieutenant in the British Army and who had been previously admitted to the Order of Merit in the second class, was elevated to the rare distinction of the 1st class. Jemadars Ramteroz and Bisram, who held commissions equivalent to second lieutenant, were promoted and granted Membership of the 2nd class. Jemadar Hunnoman Sing was similarly promoted and admitted to the Order of Merit but, unlike the two other Jemadars, he did not achieve their distinction of a triple reward (promotion, plus the OM, plus the OBI).

Subadar Adjoodhya Pattuk, Bengal Sappers & Miners. A Havildar (Sergeant) at the time of Delhi, he fought at the Kashmir Gate as one of Duncan Home's 'explosion party'. He was rewarded with admission to the 3rd Class of the (Indian) Order of Merit. Subsequently he served at the recapture of Lucknow and then in the Second China War. The precise date of his death is not known, but his military service extended from 1841 to 1876 and it would seem that he was still alive in the reign of King Edward VII. A Brahman from Oudh, he attained the highest commissioned rank then open to an Indian and was the last survivor of the Kashmir Gate attack. In this water-colour by Alex Kirk he proudly wears his old uniform and displays his medals. The necklace is made of beads or narwhal teeth. It has no special significance, neither religious nor military. Simply an item of self-adornment, it is worn by an old soldier who wishes to mark an important moment in his life – sitting for his portrait. (National Army Museum)

There is no proof, of course, but one cannot avoid the thought that the scale of rewards was something more than the accustomed recognition of personal courage and soldierly virtue. The British may have also wished to express their heartfelt gratitude that these Indians had remained true to their salt.

Whatever the truth, it is important that we should today recognise the Order of Merit (at least in the 1st class) as having been a decoration which was in every way comparable with the more famous bronze cross instituted by Queen Victoria.

The OM (and the OBI) underwent various amendments over the following decades before being finally phased out: the full history of these two fine Orders can be studied elsewhere. However, as though to prove that history does indeed repeat itself, the first OM awards ever granted were a consequence of the assault on the Kabul Gate at the powerful fortress of Ghazni, an Afghan stronghold on the road from Kabul to Kandahar. There, on 23 July 1839, a volunteer 'explosion party' went forward under heavy fire and laid 300 pounds of powder before the heavy wooden doors. The subsequent explosion enabled Lieutenant General Keane's attacking force to storm and capture the place (it also injured several members of the 'explosion party').

The parallels between the Kabul Gate and Kashmir Gate exploits are startling. The Ghazni party consisted of three officers (Captain A C Peat, Bombay Engineers, and Captains H M Durand and N S Macleod, Bengal Engineers), with three British non-commissioned officers, nineteen natives of the Bombay and Bengal Sappers & Miners, and a European bugler to sound the 'advance'. Peat was subsequently awarded a Brevet-Majority and a CB, but the Victoria Cross was still sixteen years in the future so the other Europeans went unrewarded. The Indian officers and

sappers, however, were eligible for the new-fangled Order of Merit which had been promulgated two years earlier but to which no admissions had yet been made. All nineteen men received the badge of the 3rd class.

The men who fought under Duncan Home at Delhi, and whose successors today still remember him as their first Commandant, were subsequently (with effect from 20 January 1858) designated the 24th Regiment (Pioneers) of Punjab Infantry. Those founder-members of the regiment made such a name for themselves, in the space of only a few weeks, that Sir John Lawrence quickly decided to order the raising of another similar formation to assist in the later battles for the suppression of the Mutiny.

On 15 September, just one day after the Kashmir Gate attack, authorisation was given for the raising of a second pioneer regiment, designated initially the 15th Regiment (Pioneers) of Punjab Infantry. The task of commanding this new formation was given to Lieutenant Robert Shebbeare VC, late of the Bengal Native Infantry and a man who had distinguished himself during the siege of Delhi. Other regiments of the Corps of Sikh Pioneers were to follow.

The Indian sappers gave outstanding service in a series of wars for which individual gallantry was recognised by numerous awards of the Order of Merit. Two particularly interesting members of the Order – Subedar Mehtab Singh and Subedar Bir Singh – each completed nearly thirty-five years' service with the 23rd Pioneers and each fought in four major campaigns (Umbeyla, Second China War, Abyssinia and Second Afghan War).

The Corps fought in the war of 1914–18 and, after a period of reorganisation, in the war of 1939–45, under the title Sikh Light Infantry (a title which they still hold today within the framework of the modern Indian Army).

APPENDIX C

The Order of British India

It will be seen from Appendix B that three of the Indian officers from the 'explosion party' were honoured not only with the Order of Merit (for gallantry) but also with admission to the Order of British India. It seems to us curious to find an instance where there was a double decoration for a single act of distinguished and courageous service. This is not normally the custom as far as the British armed services are concerned. Today we would regard it as even more remarkable for an officer to be admitted simultaneously to two separate orders and also promoted. The analogy would be the hypothetical case of a British army officer being rewarded for a single act of gallentry with a Brevet promotion, admission to the Distinguished Service Order and being made a Commander of the Bath, all at the same time. There may indeed be isolated instances where something like this has happened, but they must be regarded as exceptions to the rule.

The rules of the two new Orders appeared in the General Orders of the Commander in Chief in India upon the authority of the Governor General, Lord William Cavendish Bentinck. Details governing eligibility were published at Simla in GO 83 on 5 May and in GO 94 of 15 May 1837.

The rules of the OBI were summarised thus:

> 'This order is to be conferred by the Governor General of India in council, on native commissioned officers of the Indian army, for long, faithful, and honourable service.
>
> The 1st class to be composed exclusively of Subadars and the corresponding grades in the irregular cavalry, and limited to 100 members, with an allowance of two rupees a day each, in addition to their regimental allowances or retiring pensions.
>
> The 2nd class, of native commissioned officers indiscriminately, with the same limitation as to number, and an allowance of one rupee a day each, in addition to their usual allowances and pensions.
>
> The native officers on whom the Order of British India may be

The Order of British India, First Class, with its plain blue narrow ribbon intended to be worn about the neck. There were minor differences in the manufacture of the two classes of the Order, but the most noticeable is the absence of the Imperial Crown from the Second Class. In 1878 the rules of eligibility were broadened to admit Europeans who had given long and faithful commissioned service in the Indian Army. (Photograph by Robert J Scarlett)

> conferred, in the first instance, will be entitled to the extra allowance going with that distinction, from this date.
>
> The insignia of the order to consist of a gold star pendent from a sky blue ribbon, one inch and a half broad, to be worn round the neck on the outside of the collar of the coat, on full dress parades and other occasions of particular ceremony. In the centre of the star is to be inscribed, in English only, "the Order of British India."
>
> Subadars of the 1st class will receive the title of "Surdar Bahadoor", and native officers of the 2nd class that of "Bahadoor".'

Details were given regarding the distribution of the 100 memberships between officers of the armies of the three Presidencies (Bengal, Madras and Bombay). The limitation on membership presumably derived from the associated monetary commitment to be met each year by the John Company financial controllers. In short, there must have been a 'waiting list' in much the same way as pensioners formerly in Crown service were often obliged to wait many years before receiving their Meritorious Service medals. It is unlikely that three vacancies were conveniently available for Toola, Ramteroz and Bisram at the time of their exploit, so presumably the '100 maximum' rule was waived in the immediate aftermath of the Mutiny.

It is important to note that both Orders were founded upon a concept of 'progressive elevation'. Hence, speaking of Toola, he could receive the OM in the 1st class because he already held the 2nd class. But he could receive the OBI in the 2nd class only, never having been previously admitted into Membership of that Order. In this context the OM and OBI were analogous to the classic orders of chivalry in Europe. It can be readily understood why the recipients of these honours took such pride in them.

The prestige attaching to the awards was further enhanced by the distinctive titles granted to the officers so honoured. There is no precise equivalent in the English language, but an approximate translation for 'Sirdar' would be 'Knight' or 'Commander' (OBI in the 1st class), and for 'Bahadur' an approximation would be 'The Honourable' (OBI in the 2nd class).

Prior to 1837 outstanding service and personal bravery had been rewarded by grants of land and money, promotion, and the presentation of fine quality swords, shawls and turbans. The introduction of the OM and OBI replaced such *laissez faire* arrangements with a uniform standard throughout the John Company armies. The elaborate ceremonies and procedures attaching to them lent great dignity to these marks of distinction. The badges themselves (and it is not appropriate to describe them as 'medals') were issued without any naming on the reverse, the reason being that those of the lower class were returned to the authorities upon the elevation of the Member to a higher class, and his original badge could be then issued to a new Member.

The usefulness of an award, the number of years for which it endures, is a reliable indication of the soundness of the rules under which originally it was instigated. It is therefore interesting to find that the basic terms of the 1837 Warrant stood the test of time, and the pressures of radically changing circumstances, until 1947. It was found necessary, from time to time (1902, 1937 and 1945), to amend the design of the badge or the wording of the rules and regulations. But essentially the OBI continued to enjoy a position of respect and prestige over a period of one hundred and ten years.

As the scope of the award was broadened, so did it come to include those who were serving with 'Frontier Corps and Military Police, and of Our Royal Indian Navy and of Our Hong Kong–Singapore Artillery, and from among those on the active list of the Indian States Forces, for long, faithful and honourable service. Officers of the Indian Army holding Commissions of Our Viceroy, the Indian Officers of Indian States Forces, Frontier Corps and Military Police, and Indian Commissioned Officers and Indian Warrant Officers of Our Royal Indian Navy, and Indian Officers of Our Hong Kong–Singapore Artillery may be appointed to the Second Class. Appointments to the First Class shall be made only from members of the Second Class'.

The days when the OBI was granted primarily to elderly veterans of the old John Company armies were long past.

Needless to say, the events of 1947, when India gained her independence within the Commonwealth, signalled the demise of all such awards. There cannot now be many men still living who are entitled to wear this handsome badge. Those who do, and we must assume that they still do so with pride, are displaying a symbol of an era which will never return. Like all medals, it was a milestone in history, a marker along the pathway of progress. To hold such a symbol in one's hand today, nearly half a century after Britain's departure from the sub-continent, is to contemplate a time when the quality of a man was judged solely by the strength of his character and by his loyalty to his ideals.

APPENDIX D

Reports & Despatches

In the early hours of the morning of 14 September, soon after he had returned from his daring reconnaissance of the city's defences, Duncan Home received his written order for the attack which was due to start almost immediately:

'Memorandum for Lieutenant D. C. Home
Lieutenant Home, with Lieutenant Salkeld and four European non-commissioned officers, each carrying a 25 lb. bag of powder, will accompany the covering party of Rifles that precedes the column and will proceed to blow in the Cashmere Gate. The party will be accompanied by a bugler of the 52nd Regiment, and on the explosion causing a successful demolition, Lieutenant Home will cause the bugler to sound the regimental call, which will be a signal for the column to advance and storm the gateway.

If the demolition is not complete and the breach made quite passable, Lieutenant Home will at once send notice of the fact to Colonel Campbell, and will himself rejoin the column with his party, following the first column by the breach. If from any cause whatever no explosion should take place, intimation will at once be sent to the different divisions by Lieutenant Home.

(Signed) R. Baird Smith,
Lieutenant-Colonel, Chief Engineer

Dated Camp before Delhi, September 14, 1857.'

Subsequently Duncan wrote his formal report, describing what had happened. This report is undated, but it is apparent that it was composed after the city had fallen:

'From Lieutenant D. C. Home to Lieutenant-Colonel R. Baird Smith, Chief Engineer

Sir, – In accordance with your instructions I have the honour to forward as detailed an account as possible of the proceedings of the party ordered to blow open the Cashmere Gate of the city of Delhi on the morning of the 14th inst.

The covering party of the 60th Regiment Royal Rifles having advanced in skirmishing order from No.2 Battery (left) at Ludlow Castle, the explosion party (as per margin), provided with powder bags and ladders, proceeded to the front at the double, halting once under cover to enable stragglers to come up. On advancing again Sergeants John Smith and Carmichael, and Madho Havildar, all of the Sappers, and myself arrived at the Cashmere Gate, untouched, a short time in advance of the remainder of the party under Lieutenant Salkeld, having found the palisade gate on the outside of the ditch and the wicket of the Cashmere Gate open and three planks of the bridge across the ditch removed. As Sergeant Carmichael was laying his powder bag he was killed by a shot from the wicket. Havildar Madho was, I believe, also wounded about the same time.

Lieutenant Salkeld, carrying the slow match to light the charge, now came up with a portion of the remainder of the party, and with a view to enable him to shield himself as much as possible from the fire from the wicket, which was very severe (and the advanced party having deposited the powder bags), I slipped down into the ditch. Lieutenant Salkeld, being wounded in the leg from the wicket, handed over the match to Corporal Burgess of the Sappers, who was mortally wounded while completing the operation. Havildar Tillok was at the same time wounded while assisting Corporal Burgess into the ditch; Sepoy Rambeth was also killed at the same time. As I was assisting Lieutenant Salkeld into the ditch, I think he was wounded a second time.

The charge having exploded blew in the right (proper right) leaf of the gate, on which I caused the regimental call of the 52nd Regiment to be sounded as the signal for the advance of the storming party. As I was afraid that the bugle might not be heard, I caused the bugler to sound the call three times, after which the column advanced to the storm, and the gate was taken possession of by our troops.

I have now only to bring to your notice the gallant conduct of Lieutenant Salkeld, who was wounded while firing the charge; of Sergeant John Smith (Sappers and Miners), who arrived at the gate at the same time as myself; of Bugler Hawthorne, of the 52nd Regiment, who accompanied the party to give the signal for the advance, and who, under a heavy musketry fire, while Lieutenant Salkeld was lying wounded in the ditch, bound up his arm and leg with bandages, and exerted himself in every possible way to ease Lieutenant Salkeld; of Madho Havildar (Sappers and Miners), who arrived at the gate along with myself, and was wounded while placing the powder bags; of Tillok Havildar (Sappers and Miners), who was of Lieutenant Salkeld's party, and was wounded while assisting Corporal Burgess into the ditch; of Jahub Singh, Sepoy (Sappers and Miners), who was one of the party who came up with powder bags along with Lieutenant Salkeld; of Tooloo Ram Subadar (Sappers and Miners), who was of Lieutenant Salkeld's party and who, under a very heavy musketry fire, exerted himself on relieving Lieutenant Salkeld's Jemadars. I regret exceedingly that Government has lost the services of Sergeant Carmichael and Corporal Burgess of the Sappers and Miners, who were killed before the fire from the wicket, two more gallant men than whom it is difficult to meet with.

I have now given as succinct and correct an account of our proceedings as the excitement and bustle of the moment would allow me to achieve, and I hope that the conduct of the whole detachment under my orders will meet with your approbation. After the gate was blown in we ought to have advanced with the third assault column towards the Jumna Musjid, but we unluckily missed the column and only joined it in the Bank Compound.

I have the honour to be, &c.
(Signed) D. C. Home, Lieutenant Engineers.'

Baird Smith was unstinting in his praise for Duncan and his party when describing the events in his own report to the GOC, Sir Archdale Wilson:

'The gallantry with which the explosion party under Lieutenants Home and Salkeld performed the desperate duty of blowing up the Cashmere Gate in broad daylight in face of the enemy will, I feel sure, be held to justify me in making mention of it.'

He went on to say:

'I feel certain that a single statement of this devoted and glorious deed will suffice to stamp it as one of the noblest on record in military history. Its perfect success contributed most materially to the brilliant result of the day, and Lieutenants Home and Salkeld with their gallant subordinates, European and native, will, I doubt not, receive the reward to which valour before the enemy so distinguished as theirs has entitled them.'

Baird Smith also stated:

'The Punjab Sappers and Miners under their Commandant, Lieut. Gulliver (of whose valuable service I was deprived during the siege by his severe illness) and their Acting Commandant, Lieut. Home, have done excellent service, and give the best possible promise of being an efficient and soldier-like corps.'

The officer commanding the third assault column gave full credit to the party which had prepared the way for his own attack:

> 'From Colonel G. Campbell, Commanding Her Majesty's 52nd Foot, and in command of the 3rd Column of Assault, to the Adjutant-General of the Army, – dated Delhi, 16th September 1857.
>
> I have the honour to report, for the information of the Major-General, the operations of the 3rd Column of Assault, which was under my command, on the morning of the 14th instant.
>
> It consisted of 240 of Her Majesty's 52nd Regiment, 500 of the 1st Punjab Infantry, and 260 of the Kumaon Battalion. On the order for the several columns to advance, the explosion party at once proceeded towards the Cashmere Gate, upon which they advanced with most fearless intrepidity. The explosion was accomplished successfully; but I regret to say that out of the seven brave officers and men who composed it, five of them fell. Immediately upon the report of the explosion, the storming party, consisting of a company of Her Majesty's 52nd Regiment, under the command of Captain Bailey, advanced with a cheer, and overcoming all resistance, speedily secured the gateway; the supports, consisting of fifty men of Her Majesty's 52nd Regiment, fifty of the Kumaon Battalion, and fifty of the 1st Punjab Infantry, followed the storming party at a distance of fifty yards. The entire column having entered the main guard, and re-formed as speedily as possible, proceeded to carry out the orders issued by the Major-General.'

Campbell concluded his report with these words:

> 'It is difficult to select individuals from the ranks, where all behaved so well, who may have particularly distinguished themselves; but I have no hesitation in specifying the following non-commissioned officers and soldiers as deserving of particular reward, viz the non-commissioned officers of the Sappers and Miners who formed the explosion party; Sergeant-Major Streets of the 52nd, whose gallant conduct was conspicuous up to the time that he was severely wounded; Bugler Robert Hawthorn, 52nd, who accompanied the explosion party, who sounded the signal to advance, and assisted and bound up the wounds of Lieutenant Salkeld, and carried him to the rear without further injury; Lance-Corporal Henry Smith of the 52nd, for gallant conduct in carrying a wounded comrade across the Chandnee Chouk, under a tremendous fire of grape and musketry; Lance-Corporal William Taylor of the 52nd, for conspicuous gallantry throughout the operations.'

The Governor General of India, Lord Canning, in his despatch at the conclusion of the battle, paid his own tribute:

'Where so much has been done to merit admiration, it is difficult to select acts for particular notice . . . but that no injustice will be done if he offer a tribute of admiration and thanks to the brave soldiers who under Lieuts. Salkeld and Home accomplished the desperate task of blowing in the Kashmir Gate . . . It will be the care of the Governor-General that the brave men, both European and Native, who survived to share the glory of it shall not go unrewarded, and that the memory of those who fell shall be honoured.'

Mention of Lord Canning, a political appointee, shifts the focus of our attention from India to England. Inevitably, the tremendous shock of the Mutiny had profound political implications at Westminster. The Prime Minister of the day was Viscount Palmerston, a skilled politician and former Foreign Secretary who was, nonetheless, relatively new to the supreme office. He had inherited a national and international situation in many ways unstable and potentially dangerous. Great Britain had not long emerged from a troublesome war in South Africa, a disastrous campaign in the Crimea, a minor war in Persia, and was still struggling to establish herself in China. The relationship with France was worse than it had been at any time since the Revolutionary and Napoleonic wars of 1793–1814, there was trouble in Ireland, and England's industrial heartland was unsettled by the emergence of the trade union movement.

The only stable element in Britain's world affairs had been India, where Lord Dalhousie served as Governor General from 1848 to 1856, exerting a remarkable influence upon the modernisation of the sub-continent. He introduced important social, economic and judicial reforms. He also concluded the annexation of the Punjab (1849), Pegu (1852) and Oudh (1856). Unfortunately, the speed of his reforms was such that Indian susceptibilities were offended and the story of the 'greased cartridges' was given credence when otherwise it might have been rejected. Worse, Dalhousie had been replaced by another Governor General, Lord Canning, an able, intelligent and humane administrator, but one who was as new to his post as Palmerston was to 10 Downing Street.

It was inevitable that Canning should be the target for outraged criticism, it being alleged that he had permitted the onset of the Mutiny and failed to prevent the appalling atrocities. Those who wished to bring down Palmerston's government siezed upon Canning's conduct of his office as the tool for their purpose. Palmerston, on the other hand, wished to justify his government's policy toward India and to demonstrate his apparent confidence in Canning's administration.

Palmerston could do little to defend himself in 1857 because the news arriving from India was consistently disastrous. However, at the turn of the year, detailed reports of the triumph at Delhi started to reach London.

The time had come for the Prime Minister to strike back at his critics. The Christmas recess ended, he found an early opportunity to bring before the House of Commons a motion for the adoption of 'a vote of thanks to the civil service, army and navy in India'. The motion was introduced at short notice and it aroused the fury of the opposition. They did not dispute the courage and resource of the officers and men who were fighting to contain the Mutiny and to defeat the mutineers, but they objected strongly to the inclusion of Canning's name. Some held him directly responsible for the catastrophe, others held that it would be improper to include his name in such a resolution without first having all the facts before them.

The motion was introduced to the Commons by the Prime Minister on the evening of 8 February 1858. At the same time, across the lobby, a similar motion was debated in the House of Lords. It should be noted that these 'votes of thanks' by Parliament were matters of notable rarity and importance. They were official marks of approbation by Parliament, reflecting all shades of political and national opinion, in respect of the services of Great Britain's generals and admirals for their conduct in a particular campaign or war. As precedents we have, amongst others, the examples of Parker and Nelson (1801) for Copenhagen; Saumarez (1801) for Gibraltar; Wellesley, Clive and Lake (1804) for India; Gambier (1810) for Basque Roads; Wellington (1814) at the conclusion of the war with France; and Exmouth (1817) for Algiers.

Both Houses were unanimous in wishing to show their appreciation of the services of the officers and men who had fought at Delhi and Lucknow; what annoyed Palmerston's critics was his device of including the name of Canning in the draft of the resolution at the last moment. Disraeli was particularly scathing in his speech, drawing a comparison between the fortitude of men such as Inglis and Havelock on the one hand, and the alleged incompetence of Canning on the other. At the end of a long and near acrimonious debate, the full wording proposed by Palmerston was adopted unanimously:

> 'Resolved, Nemine Contradicente, that the thanks of this House be given to the Right Honourable Viscount Canning, Governor General of the British Possessions in the East Indies; the Right Honourable

Archdale Wilson's extraordinary victory at Delhi – when less than 5,000 men stormed one of the most powerfully fortified places in India and overcame an enemy at least three times more numerous – caught the imagination of the British public and inspired a wave of artistic acclaim. This beautiful and detailed oil painting, by W S Morgan, was a typical response. That the picture is totally inaccurate is of little importance compared with the artist's enthusiasm for his subject. (National Army Museum)

Lord Harris, Governor of the Presidency of Madras; the Right Honourable Lord Elphinstone, Governor of the Presidency of Bombay; Sir John Laird Mair Lawrence, G.C.B., Chief Commissioner of the Punjaub; and Henry Bartle Edward Frere, Esquire, Commissioner of Scinde, for the energy and ability with which they have employed the resources at their command to suppress the widely-spread mutiny in Her Majesty's Indian Dominions.

Resolved, Nemine Contradicente, that the thanks of this House be given to His Excellency General Sir Colin Campbell, G.C.B., Commander in Chief in India; Major General Sir James Outram, G.C.B.; Major General Sir Archdale Wilson, Baronet, K.C.B.; and Major General Sir John Eardley Wilmot Inglis, K.C.B., for the eminent skill, courage, and perseverance displayed by them in the achievement of so many and such important triumphs over numerous bodies of the mutineers.

Resolved, Nemine Contradicente, that the thanks of this House be given to the other gallant officers of Her Majesty's army, navy, and marines; and also of the Honourable East India Company's Service, for the intrepidity, the patient endurance, and other high military qualities which have marked their discharge of those arduous duties which they have so successfully performed.

Resolved, Nemine Contradicente, that this House doth highly approve and acknowledge the high courage, the devoted loyalty, and

the brilliant services of the non-commissioned officers and men of Her Majesty's military and naval forces; of the European troops in the service of the Honourable East India Company; and of the great body of those Native Corps throughout India who have remained faithful to their standards; and that the same be signified to them by the commanders of the several corps, who are desired to thank them for their gallant behaviour.

Resolved, Nemine Contradicente, that this House doth highly appreciate and cordially approve of the course, self-devotion, and exemplary conduct of those persons, who, though not holding military rank, have nevertheless performed valuable military service in the field, or in defence of various posts throughout the disturbed districts in India at which they were resident; and that the Governor General be requested to thank these persons for their spirited and patriotic exertions.'

A resolution, of similar wording, was adopted by the House of Lords and, for the moment, the government survived intact. Only a few days later, however, Palmerston ran into much greater difficulty with regard to his policy towards the French. His government fell and he was succeeded as Prime Minister by Lord Derby.

We may be grateful for the contention then rife in political circles because, instead of going through 'on the nod' (a unanimous 'silent vote'), Palmerston's motion was debated at length. A number of points emerged from the speeches which are relevant to the history of the assault on Delhi. Indeed, the speeches from each side of the House of Commons were analogous to those made by counsel in a court of law. Canning's reputation was placed, albeit inadvertently, on trial. Each side strove to make its point by citing various instances of either skilful foresight, or gross mismanagement, depending upon the judgement of the speaker. Consequently, instead of finding in Hansard the expected formal laudatory references to the highest ranking individuals only, we discover the names of the very junior officers and men who figure in the story of the Kashmir Gate.

At one point in his opening speech, the Prime Minister stated:

'Then there was General Neill, an officer of great merit, and whose death was a great loss to his country. Lieutenant Willoughby early distinguished himself by one of the most daring attempts ever made, and, although when he blew up the magazine at Delhi he at the time escaped, he (later) fell a victim either to disease or to the assault or ambuscades of the enemy. Then there was Salkeld, whose name in conjunction with that of Lieutenant Home will go down in posterity as that of men who, in the performance of a desperate duty, blowing in the gate of Delhi, displayed a cool judgement and an indifference to danger which have never been surpassed. Well, Sir, there have been many others whose names I forebear from enumerating, but whose services we ought not upon the present occasion to forget.'

Palmerston returned to this theme later in the same speech:

'There is Colonel Jones, of the 31st Foot, who made himself conspicuous at Delhi; Colonel Campbell, of the 32nd [*sic*], and Colonel Jones, of the 60th, who also distinguished themselves on the same occasion. Colonel Baird Smith, of the Engineers, had the merit of conducting, under General Wilson, all the siege operations of Delhi with the greatest ability, and succeeded in placing a battery within fifty [*sic*] yards of the wall to be breached, a feat worthy of the highest admiration. Lieutenant Raynor and Lieutenant Forrest co-operated with Lieutenant Willoughby in that gallant exploit of blowing up the magazine at Delhi.'

When Palmerston sat down he was followed by Benjamin Disraeli, speaking from the opposition front bench. Disraeli, having made generous references to all the great and famous men then serving in India, and having said that he did not intend to enter at that time into any controversy with regard to the conduct of Lord Canning, proceeded to do precisely that. In a speech of the greatest subtlety he listed all of the counts upon which the Governor General was currently charged in the press and in the corridors of power.

Disraeli was followed by other speakers, most of their remarks being addressed to the disputed competence of Canning rather than the valour of the armies in the field.

It was a back-bencher, Colonel W H Sykes, formerly of the Bombay Army and formerly Chairman of John Company, who tried to bring the House back to the main purpose of the debate by calling its attention to an error which had appeared in several newspapers. More than one journalist had reported Salkeld as the leader of the 'explosion party', with Home his second-in-command. Further, at least one newspaper stated that Duncan Home had been killed at the Kashmir Gate and that Philip Salkeld had survived. Colonel Sykes explained to the House the true facts of the case.

Not surprisingly, it was a former sailor, Admiral Walcott, who paid tribute to the role of Captain Peel's naval brigade in assisting in the suppression of the Mutiny.

Sir de Lacy Evans complained that so few officers were named individually in the resolution under debate, and pointed out that the brunt of the fighting had been borne by officers of comparatively junior rank.

He also expressed the view 'when Delhi was taken, the neck of the revolt was completely broken.'

One of the most uninhibited speeches came from General Thompson, who had himself served in India, and who deplored the arrogance of 'the European immigrants or colonists, who brought from the slave pens of America that detestable term which is among gentlemen *non nominandum*'. Thompson had a good point; there had been no colour prejudice for more than two centuries but, with the ascendency of Victorian social attitudes, the contemptuous 'nigger' and 'blacks' started to appear in correspondence from India to England. Thompson was equally bitter regarding the alleged use of the prohibited tallow on the cartridges: 'the only means by which the Indian soldier can be driven into resistance is by attacking him in his religion – the free exercise of which was guaranteed to him when he enlisted. Why could they not let the Indian army alone? Why did they insist on filling the mouths of the soldiers with hog's lard? If the Lifeguards or the Blues were invited to trample on the Cross, or the Connaught Rangers to do what they considered the equivalent to spitting on the Host . . . the same kind of results would follow.'

The debate dragged on, and it became evident that the House was determined not to permit the government to 'smuggle through a mark of approval for Canning's administration'. Viscount Palmerston bowed to the inevitable and agreed that the inclusion of the Governor General's name in the resolution 'showed that the thanks were intended to apply simply to the measures taken by Lord Canning in support of the military operations, and had no reference to the general policy of the government'. It was game, set and match to Disraeli.

Meanwhile, a few yards away, the House of Lords conducted its own debate on an identical resolution. The course of this debate mirrored that in the Commons but, as might be expected, the quality of the speeches was both more restrained and oratorically more appealing. Lord Panmure, Secretary of State for War, in proposing the resolution, spoke eloquently and at great length. The following extracts are of relevance to our story, and the first contains a generous tribute to the General Officer Commanding, Delhi Field Force:

'I now come to another name which I am sure your Lordships will be

All the main features of Delhi are apparent in this pre-Mutiny sketch. From left to right: the Jumna river and the pontoon bridge; the enclosure of the Royal Palace (the Red Fort); the Chandi Chouk or Street of Silver (bisecting the city from left to right); the Jumma Musjid in the middle distance (the great Muslim temple); and the northern wall where the British attacked. The open area in the lower right-hand corner was the site of the final assault.

disposed to regard as one which ought to occupy a prominent place upon this occasion. It is that of Major General Sir Archdale Wilson, the conqueror of Delhi. In adverting to that gallant General I may be permitted to remark that the honours of the struggle in which we have been engaged in India do not altogether belong to the officers in Her Majesty's service, but are shared by those who are employed in the service of the Company. Sir Archdale Wilson commenced his career some years ago in that service, and was in command, at the time of the outbreak of the mutiny, in the district of the Punjab. The division of which he was at the head was destined to join the army which was ordered to advance to the siege of Delhi. When he arrived in the vicinity of that city he found himself second in command to Sir Henry Barnard, and his first operations against the fortress consisted of a combined movement with that gallant General, which combined movement he executed with a skill that gave the strongest evidence of his capacity, and clearly presaged the glory which crowned his subsequent career. The movement to which I refer enabled Sir Henry Barnard to conquer and to occupy in one day that most important position which was subsequently held by our army before Delhi, and from which operations were conducted with an advantage to which it is to be attributed that

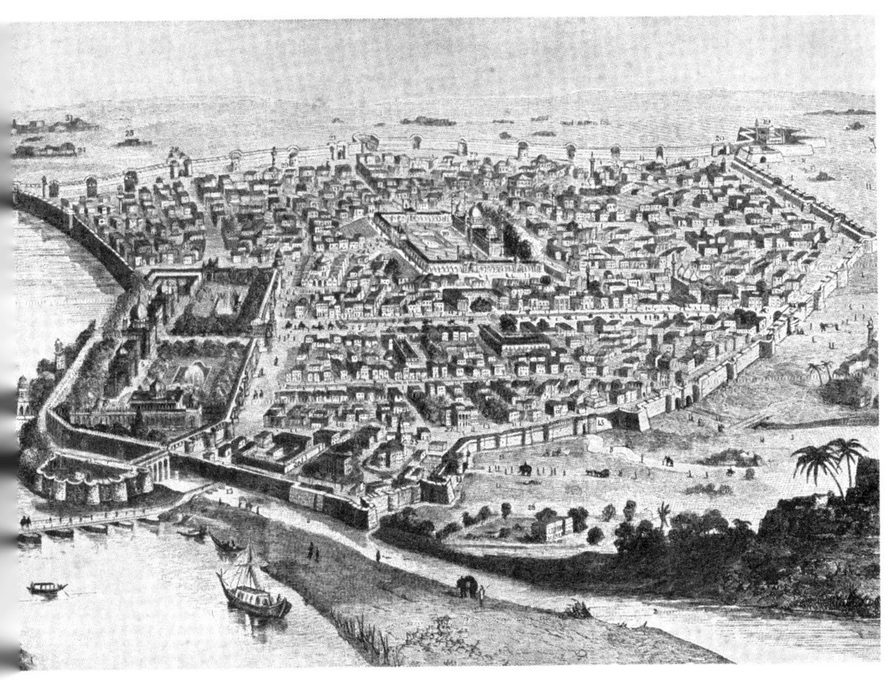

the siege of that city was not still further prolonged. After the death of the gallant and lamented Sir Henry Barnard the chief command fell to the lot of Major General Wilson. He then, with a coolness, deliberation, and judgment which merit our praise, deferred making an assault upon the fortress until he should find himself sufficiently reinforced to be able to do so with a probability of success. He knew perfectly well the effect which failure in the attempt to take Delhi would produce among the native population of India. He paused, therefore, until he could operate with advantage, and when he found himself in a position which rendered success feasible, he achieved the great object which he had in view, and achieved it in a manner which clearly proved that he is eminently well qualified to discharge the arduous duties which attach to an officer in high command. But, my Lords, while General Wilson was waiting for reinforcements before Delhi, the army under him was by no means idle. He covered their position with great skill and attended to the comfort of his troops in a way which was well repaid by their devotion, as was testified by the success with which they assaulted the enemy and repelled the attacks made upon them upon no less than twenty-six or twenty-seven different occasions. Then came the final triumph. Delhi was captured, and I am sure your Lordships will deeply sympathize with its conqueror, who immediately after this great success had been achieved was obliged, owing to the state of his health, to retire for a season from active military command. Let us hope, my Lords, that it is only for a season, and that he will soon be able to return with increased vigour to the service of his country. In the meantime no better panacea can, I am sure, be administered for the restoration of his infirm and broken constitution than those thanks which I feel confident your Lordships will cordially and unanimously accord him.'

Panmure described the services of several other field commanders before making a personal tribute to Sir Henry Lawrence. He continued:

'I think, therefore, the name of Sir Henry Lawrence deserves the warmest sympathies of your Lordships. I may further mention the names of Neill, Wheeler, and Nicholson, and, descending to inferior ranks, those of Salkeld, Home, and Willoughby. Of General Neill I can state that he was as gallant and distinguished a soldier as I have ever known. I had the honour of his personal acquaintance . . .'

Lord Panmure continued to work his way dutifully through the list of senior commanders, with some affectionate remarks for the kindly old General Anson, before reaching that part of his speech which was, by the standards of the day, exceptional:

'I might allude to the names of Colonel Finnis and of other officers whom we lost during the mutiny; but I will only refer to those gallant and illustrious men – Home, Salkeld, and Willoughby – who rendered the most important services. Lieutenant Willoughby by destroying, at his own peril, the resources of the enemy and endeavouring to prevent large stores of ammunition from falling into his hands, and Lieutenants Salkeld and Home by undertaking to blow open the gates of Delhi. I will not do more than mention their names, but it is impossible to pass by this last exploit without singling out and mentioning, in conjunction with Home and Salkeld, Sergeants Carmichael and Smith, and the bugler who engaged with them in the bold attempt which cost those gallant men their lives [*sic*].

There are many others who have sacrificed their lives in putting down the Indian mutiny, but I will not detain your Lordships by entering further into the subject. I will simply conclude the observations I have thought it necessary to address to you by submitting to your Lordships an additional Resolution which is not included among those of which I have given notice. I trust that, in undertaking to bring before you this very wide, and in some respects very difficult subject, I shall not, by any omission I have made, occasion pain, which assuredly I am most anxious to avoid giving, to the mind of any gallant soldier. Your Lordships will, I hope, understand, that in submitting these Resolutions I propose to thank the whole Army which has been concerned in the suppression of the mutinies in India. I propose to thank every Private and every Non-commissioned Officer, as well as every Officer in the service. I have named the Generals as supreme in command; I have mentioned others who are well known, and whose deeds are familiar to the public; but I entreat your Lordships to give to all the meed of your thanks, and to adopt the Resolutions which I shall have the honour of placing in the hands of the Lord Chancellor.'

A cynic might regard the second part of this quotation – the reference to 'every private soldier . . .' – as nothing more than a token nod in the direction of egalitarian democracy. Panmure was fully aware of the need to make a favourable impression upon all levels of national sentiment. But the first part of the extract, the direct reference to John Smith and Andrew Carmichael, even the indirect reference to Bugler Hawthorne, was certainly a novelty of the first magnitude. In an age when the gulf between the various social classes was immense, an age when the common soldiery was held to be part of the lower orders, we can only wonder that a senior member of the Cabinet should have felt moved to mention them by name in the House of Lords.

It should be noted that only five junior officers were identified during the debates in the House of Commons and the House of Lords.

Lieutenants Willoughby, Forrest and Raynor were praised for their near-suicidal attempt to destroy the magazine at Delhi when the mutineers tried to occupy it on 11 May. Forrest and Raynor were subsequently awarded the Victoria Cross, but the unfortunate Willoughby, having survived the explosion and having escaped from the city, was murdered by villagers while trying to make his way to Meerut. His only reward was the frequent reference to his name in the debates at Westminster nine months later.

Literally hundreds of heroic episodes occurred in various parts of northern India during the course of the Mutiny. That the Kashmir Gate affair was singled out for special mention at Westminster is a fair measure of the importance attaching to its success. A further year would pass before the disturbances finally came to an end, there were many hard battles yet to be fought, but already the authorities in India and the politicians in England could recognise that the tide had turned. Sir de Lacy Evans' remark was highly perceptive: 'when Delhi was taken, the neck of the revolt was completely broken'. It is not difficult to understand why Palmerston and Panmure both identified Duncan Home and Philip Salkeld as key figures, and why Panmure made his unprecedented reference to the three soldiers who served under them.

APPENDIX E

The Home Family

Duncan Charles Home came from a family which traces its origins back through the pages of English history to the year AD 1000. A union between the families of King Duncan of Scotland and King Ethelred of England gave rise to the Earldom of Dunbar. Two hundred years later, early in the thirteenth century, a cousin of Patricius, sixth Earl of Dunbar, received the estates of Home as a dowry and so established the family name of de Home. Each succeeding generation added to the power and prestige of this line until, in 1390, Sir Thomas de Home emerged as one of the most influential landowners in Northumbria. He was the common ancestor of all the various families of Home which still exist today and they all devolve from the foundation which he created in the shire of Berwick.

There were five principal collateral families. One was enobled in 1473 and produced the long succession of the Earls of Home. The former Prime Minister of Great Britain, Sir Alec Douglas Home, now the Lord Home of The Hirzel KT, is a member of this branch. The next was that of Wedderburn, followed by that of Polwarth (which was also enobled and generated the Earls of Marchmont). A fourth and short-lived branch was that of Coldingham-Law, while that to which Duncan Home belonged was the Greenlaw Castle branch.

Duncan's grandfather was Robert Home, a surgeon's son born in Hull in 1752, a remarkable and talented man whose career was far from typical of the traditions from which he sprang. A wild-spirited boy with a crippled left arm, he ran away from school and went to sea as cabin-boy in a whaler. Returning from Newfoundland he convinced his parents that they should permit him to develop his natural skill as an artist. He went to Rome to study painting and then tried to earn a living as a portraitist in London. Finding the competition too stiff he moved to Dublin and was soon established in fashionable society. He acquired a profitable clientèle, married, and settled for several years, but then his restless temperament led him on to new adventures. Leaving his wife and children in London,

A self-portrait by Robert Home (1752–1834). It is undated but, judged by his appearance, it is probable that he made this portrait during the early 1800s in Calcutta. (National Portrait Gallery)

he travelled to India in 1789 and attached himself (as official artist) to the staff of Lord Cornwallis during the Third Mysore War. This unusual appointment brought Robert Home into contact with men of great importance, one of whom was Sir Arthur Wellesley (later the Duke of Wellington). The two became friends and the Iron Duke later sat for three portraits by the artist.

Major General Sir Arthur Wellesley (later the Duke of Wellington), 1769–1852. He marked his great victory at Assaye by commissioning Robert Home to paint his portrait. The work was done in the artist's Calcutta studio in 1804. Wellesley's appointment as a Knight of the Bath was not notified in India until 1805, hence the great soldier is not wearing his Star in this picture. (National Portrait Gallery)

A fine study in oils by Robert Home from the Third Mysore War: 'The reception of the Mysore princes by Lord Cornwallis'. In February 1792, Cornwallis and Abercrombie besieged Tipu Sultan's island capital of Seringapatam, forcing the Mysorean into making peace. John Company gained control of the whole of Malabar and Coorg. As a guarantee of the peace treaty, Tipu agreed to place two of his sons in Cornwallis's care. This stylish picture displays not only the artist's great skill as a portraitist, but also his impish sense of humour. He had personally witnessed the event so, when later he came to paint the scene, he included himself (extreme left, holding portfolio) in the crowd of spectators. (National Army Museum)

At the end of the campaign Robert Home found himself at a loose end. He travelled throughout India, obtaining commissions as and where he could, and then settled in Calcutta in 1795. His wife had died in London soon after her husband's departure for India, but now the children were brought out to join their father. They were accompanied by the family nurse. Robert married her and they lived in Calcutta until 1814 when they moved to Lucknow to join the Court of the King of Oudh. Sitters for portraits had become scarce and, in need of regular income, Robert accepted the appointment of State Painter. His four adolescent sons were granted cadetships in the service of the East India Company and two of them were attached to the Royal entourage. They all lived happily in the palace of the King for eleven years until, following the death of their

Duncan Home's younger brother, Robert, photographed in 1856 when he was employed at Saharanpore on the construction of the Eastern Jumna canal. Born in Calcutta in 1834, he served thirty-three years with the Bengal Engineers and (after 1862) with the Royal Engineers. He died in 1896 in the rank of Colonel, CIE. (Photograph by kind permission of Mrs Margaret Home-Tucker)

employer, their position became precarious and they moved in 1825 to Cawnpore.

Robert Home died nine years later, in modest circumstances, but having lived a very full life and having safely launched his sons into their military careers. He was eighty-two years of age at the time of his death and he was laid to rest in the Katcheri Cemetery, Cawnpore. Regarded as the 'black sheep' of the family by his relations in England (painting not being thought a suitable occupation for a gentleman), he was the man whose maverick nature had brought the name of Home to India. His descendants were to give much valuable service to that country over the following decades.

His four sons, all born in Dublin, each had interesting careers of varying fortune. The eldest, also named Robert, was born in 1784. Not long after his arrival in India he joined the Madras Army as a cadet. In 1805 he made a sea voyage with one of his younger brothers, Richard, who had been ill and had been prescribed a convalescent cruise to aid his recovery. Their ship was captured by a French frigate and the two young officers were held prisoner on Mauritius for eighteen months before being exchanged. Robert later took part in the capture of Mauritius, the expedition to Java, the battle of Assaye and the conquest of Ava (Burma). He became a Commander of the Bath and died in 1842.

The second son, William James, born in 1786, joined the Madras Army and died at Aurangabad in 1809 from the effects of a wound received in action three years earlier. The third, John, born in 1787, joined the Bengal Army as a cadet and for some years commanded the Royal Bodyguard at

the Court of the King of Oudh. He later rose to the rank of Major General, retired to England, and died in Bath in 1860.

The fourth son, Richard, born in 1789, followed John into the Bengal Army as a cadet attached to the King of Oudh's staff and for a while commanded the Resident's Escort. After his father's retirement he joined the 13th Bengal Native Infantry (which he eventually commanded) and served at Lucknow, Cawnpore and Jubbalpore. His marriage produced

Lieutenant Edward Trevor Hume (1837–1913), another of Duncan Home's distant cousins who took part in the suppression of the Mutiny. The son of George and Elizabeth Anne Hume, he was born on 9 April 1837 at 8 Great James Street, Bedford Row, London. His father obtained the prestigious appointment of Chief Clerk to the Master of the Rolls and the family moved to the fashionable address of 20 Dorset Square, Regent's Park. Edward obtained a commission in the Bengal Artillery, passing out of Addiscombe on 12 December 1856. Unusually, he travelled to India overland, arriving in Calcutta on 21 April 1857 (just as the Mutiny was surfacing). Sent to Meerut, he arrived there after the murders and was employed for some weeks in guarding the cantonment. Then, as the siege of Delhi approached its climax, he was sent south with a detachment of raw artillery recruits to reinforce Wilson's depleted force on the Ridge. He fought throughout the battle to re-occupy Delhi with 1st Company 4th Battalion Bengal Artillery, and was then sent on sick leave to the hill station of Mussoorie until January 1858. Subsequently appointed to 3rd Troop 3rd Brigade Bengal Horse Artillery, he was in the actions at Shahjahanpur and Rohilkand and the capture, on 8 November 1858, of Mithauli Fort. He retired in June 1890, after thirty-four years' service, as Colonel RA. (India Office Library & Records)

thirteen children, the first three of whom all died before reaching their first birthdays. The fourth child, born while the regiment was at Jubbalpore, was Duncan Charles – the boy who later won fame and glory at the Kashmir Gate.

Other sons rose to high rank in the Indian Army and the Indian Forestry Service. One of the most interesting of these men was yet another Robert (grandson of the artist and born in 1834) who followed Duncan into the Bengal Engineers. Like Duncan, he too was employed in the construction of canals. His career neatly illustrates the type of benefit which Great Britain was able to bring to the peoples of India. In 1856 he assisted in the building of the Eastern Jumna Canal and was stationed at Saharanpore during the Mutiny (an area undisturbed by the troubles). In 1857 he took over the appointment held previously by Duncan and for the next ten years worked on the Bari Doab Canal. In 1867 he commenced his major project, the Sirhind Canal, and remained with it until its opening in 1882 (when he was appointed a Companion of the Indian Empire). Promoted to the post of Inspector General of Irrigation in India, he retired in 1889 in the rank of Colonel and having devoted thirty-three years of his life exclusively to the Punjab waterway system. His wife presented him with seven children, of whom four were sons and all became professional soldiers. The eldest, the fourth Robert in the line, won the DSO with the Royal Artillery in the Great War. The second son, Richard, died of enteric fever at Omdurman in 1899, and the two other sons, John and William, both served with distinction with the Indian Army.

As a footnote to the story of Duncan Home, it is an interesting coincidence that he had a distant cousin who also won the Victoria Cross during the Indian Mutiny. Anthony Dickson Home was a Scot, born in 1824 at Dunbar, who qualified as a medical practitioner before entering the army as a Surgeon. He served in the Crimean campaign with the 8th and 13th Hussars. He then sailed for India with the 90th Regt (Perthshire Light Infantry) and joined the column led by General Sir Henry Havelock in the attempt to relieve the besieged garrison in the Residency at Lucknow. During this desperate venture it happened that some of the wounded and stragglers became detached from the main column and were surrounded by mutineers. They took refuge in a house until it was set on fire and then barricaded themselves in a shed. All the other officers were *hors de combat*, so Anthony Home personally maintained a fierce defence of his wounded charges until rescued twenty-two hours later. Like most army doctors of that period, he was well able to pick up a rifle or sabre when the need arose.

This gallant affair took place on 26 September 1857, just twelve days after Duncan Home won his Victoria Cross at Delhi, but the Surgeon was the luckier of the two – he lived to receive his decoration. Subsequently he served in the China war of 1857–60, the New Zealand war of 1860–66, and the Ashanti campaign of 1873–74. He was knighted (KCB) and promoted to the rank of Surgeon General. He served as Principal Medical Officer in Cyprus and India before retiring in 1886. He died in London, full of years and honours, on 10 August 1914, one week after the outbreak of 'the war to end all wars'.

The armorial bearings of the different branches of the Home family vary in matters of detail, one from the other, but it is appropriate that they all share a common motto – 'True to the End'.

APPENDIX F

Philip Salkeld VC

He was born on 13 October 1830, the fourth son of the thirteen children of a hard-working country cleric. His father was the Reverend Robert Salkeld MA, and his mother was Elizabeth Henriette, youngest daughter of Lieutenant Colonel John Wilson of the Royal Hospital, Chelsea.

The Reverend Salkeld was the incumbent of the Parish of Fontmell Magna, a small village near Shaftesbury in Dorset. He was first introduced to this incumbency by his widowed mother, Ann Salkeld of the nearby Manor of Fifehead Neville, in 1819, soon after Robert was ordained. He served the Parish for the next forty-six years, until his death, at the age of seventy, on 26 January 1866. It is possible that he may have been absent for part of this time, living in France and leaving the Parish in the charge of his curate. The family papers contain an invitation, dated May 1849, addressed to 'Rev Robert Salkeld ... St Servan ... et sa famille', to the funeral of Frederic, Comte de Chateaubriand. It is known that the Salkeld family did not in the event attend this funeral, but the evidence does at least suggest a close acquaintanceship. Hence there is the possibility that Philip may have passed a part of his youth in France.

The unusual family name of Salkeld has its roots in Cumberland. Prior to the Great Civil War of 1642–9, the family owned land in the vicinity of Penrith but, as a result of the war, the properties were lost. A century earlier, however, one branch of the family had moved to Northumberland and remained there until the early eighteenth century when, 'having married into some estates', the name was established in Dorset. Unfortunately, none of that wealth was to be found in the Rectory at Fontmell Magna. Philip's parents were hard-pressed to find the fees for his education at Dr Bridgman's School, Woolwich, where boys were prepared for a military career.

He was an intelligent lad and, in an age when personal influence was paramount, his father was fortunate in attracting the interest of William Astell, a Member of Parliament and a Director of the East India Company. Astell agreed to act as patron and sponsor to Philip. His interview for entry into the Military Seminary at Addiscombe was successful. He applied himself diligently to the curriculum and gained top prizes in mathematics and modern languages (and the latter item again raises the unanswered question regarding the Chateaubriand connection).

He entered the tough examination for selection as a potential engineer – a branch to which only the brightest youngsters were admitted – and was successful in this also. On 9 June 1848, he followed in the footsteps of Duncan Home and entered the Royal Engineer establishment at Chatham, with the rank of Second Lieutenant, for specialist training in 'the theoretic and practical study of fortification and other kindred subjects'. Completing his training in January 1850, he embarked for India and arrived in Calcutta in June of that year. Initially he studied local languages and customs, and was then employed on various road and canal construction projects. In June 1853, he was appointed 'extra Engineer' at Meerut, and in November was given responsibility for a stretch of the Grand Trunk Road. He remained in this post until December 1856, then moved to Delhi as Executive Engineer with the Public Works Department. He was promoted to the rank of Lieutenant in August 1854.

On 11 May 1857 the Meerut mutineers came streaming across the Jumna bridge and hell broke loose on the streets of the capital city. Europeans and Eurasians, sometimes alone and sometimes with their families, tried to defend themselves or make their way to the city's principal exit, the Kashmir Gate. Several groups escaped by this route before it was closed and barred by the mutineers. Later arrivals found themselves trapped in the open area inside the Gate, in front of St James's Church and known as the Main Guard. Here they milled around, frightened and searching desperately for their relatives while armed men closed threateningly around them. Soon the butchery commenced.

Philip Salkeld was one of those who had escaped the initial killings in the centre of the city. Now he stood uncertainly with the others, his faithful manservant beside him, and watched as the first of the bodies went down under a flurry of sword cuts and musket shots. He turned and ran up the steps to the top of the Kashmir Gate bastion. Others – men, women and screaming children – followed him. Near-miss bullets smacked into the stonework, others found their mark and more bodies fell.

Several people, frantic with fear, climbed onto the parapet and launched themselves into space. They fell twenty-five feet into the outer ditch and lay there, groaning and clutching their broken limbs. The remainder, like Philip, kept their heads. The officers took off their sword belts, quickly fastened them together, formed a 'rope' and lowered themselves and some of the civilians down the outer face of the wall. They ran across the floor of the ditch and scrambled up the crumbling earthwork of

Photographed shortly before the Mutiny, sepoys and non-commissioned officers of a Bengal Native Infantry regiment pose with their long-barrelled muskets. The record states that they were men of the 13th BNI and fought against the British as Pandis. This seems unlikely. The 13th was one of the loyal native regiments which fought with outstanding courage as part of the defending force during the desperate months of the siege of Lucknow. Whatever the facts, the picture serves to illustrate the good equipment and fine soldierly bearing of the Indian infantry. (India Office Library & Records)

the counterscarp. Mutineer marksmen appeared on the walls high above them and more fugitives were shot down.

Breathless and shaken, Philip and other survivors ran through the scrub and shanties north of Delhi until, late in the evening, several of them gathered in the cellar of the ransacked mansion near the banks of the Jumna. Normally this was the residence of Sir Theophilus Metcalfe, Chief Magistrate, the man who in September played an important role as guide to the British troops during the battle to re-occupy the city.

Apart from Philip, the party consisted of four officers, two ladies and three girls (the youngest a child of nine). One of the officers was a 57-years-old Lieutenant, George Forrest, later awarded the VC for his part in the attempt to destroy the magazine in the city (*vide* Appendix J). He had been shot through the hand and was in a state of shock. The girls in the party were his daughters and one of the ladies his wife (with a bullet-hole through her shoulder).

During the next two days and nights the little band of ragged fugitives crept from cover to cover, leaving the pillaged city behind them and watch-

After the Mutiny it was decided to erect a memorial to the Bengal Engineer officers who had fallen during the conflict. An official at the India Office wrote to the Reverend Robert Salkeld, enquiring whether he could supply a portrait of his late son to be used as a guide by the sculptor. The cleric replied that Philip had never been photographed or painted, but he enclosed a sketch made from memory by one of the sisters. It was agreed that 'this was a good likeness of Philip's features' and it formed the basis for the sculptor's work. In 1983 the artist Kenneth Petrie used the memorial tablet as the basis for his own impression of the young VC winner.

ing the columns of smoke rising from the burning British cantonment buildings to the east. Philip wondered whether Pandi search parties were yet on their tracks.

They met many Indians, some hostile, some indifferent, others sympathetic and helpful. Two more army officers joined the group before it was decided to head for Meerut where, according to reports from local natives, the British were still holding out.

For the next week the party went through a series of terrifying ordeals. They forded the Ganges Canal and the fast-flowing Jumna, then set out to walk across the arid sun-scorched plain of the Doab. Philip was barefoot, having given his shoes to one of the Forrest girls. On the third day they were found by a gang of Goojars – criminal scavengers – who robbed them of their few valuables and much of their clothing. The women were searched but not molested.

Later they were found by friendly natives who took them to the village of Khekra, fifteen miles north-east of Delhi. They were given milk and chuppatties, and Mrs Forrest's wound was dressed by the village barber who poured boiling butter through the gaping wound. Subsequently it healed perfectly.

A message, written in French and asking for help, was sent by the hand of a villager to Meerut. Eventually it reached General Hewitt who, at the time, was dining with his officers. He decided that a rescue would be too difficult and threw the paper under the table.

Meanwhile, the party had travelled on to the fortified village of Hurchundpore where they were kindly received by a German Jew named Cohen. Fifty years earlier he had come to India to seek his fortune, had settled in this lonely place, married an Indian lady, and adopted the local lifestyle. Cohen was the sort of 'gone native' person for whom some of the British would not normally have had a civil word, but he gave them food, shelter and clean Indian clothing. The party slept and rested, waiting for the next move.

Help appeared finally when forty of the few remaining loyal sowars of the 3rd Cavalry, commanded by Hugh Gough and A R D Mackenzie, arrived at Hurchundpore from Meerut. These two young subalterns had ignored Hewitt and mounted their own rescue operation.

The days of wandering were over. Philip and his companions were taken the remaining miles to Meerut by bullock cart. Exhausted and covered with scratches and insect bites, they were lucky to be alive. Later accounts of their saga paid tribute to Philip's unfailing cheerfulness and good humour which helped to sustain the spirits of the group. Apart from the elderly Lieutenant Forrest, who seems to have been mentally unhinged by the experience, they had all come through the ordeal with little permanent damage. One unexpected sequel was the romance which blossomed between two of the party. Lieutenant Procter fell in love with one of the Forrest girls during that desperate week, and they were married a few months later. The fates had a less happy future in store for several of the other people in the party.

Philip swiftly recovered, obtained fresh kit, was put in charge of the defence of the School of Instruction, and then joined the column being organised by Colonel Archdale Wilson. The Colonel had been ordered to march to Bhagput and to join up with the Delhi Field Force being raised in the Punjab by the Commander-in-Chief, General the Honourable George Anson.

The Meerut column set off on 27 May and three days later encountered Pandi forces holding the iron bridge over the Hindun river (a tributary of the Jumna which crosses the line of the Meerut–Delhi road). Two fierce actions followed: the mutineers fought well against their former masters before being driven back. The engineer officers, Philip Salkeld included, assisted the artillery during these actions. He also led a reconnaissance along the river bank during the battle, and later remained behind for a while to blow up the bridge.

By 7 June the Meerut column had joined the main Delhi Field Force at Alipore, one day's march from Delhi. General Anson had died of cholera at Karnal and been replaced by Major General Sir Henry Barnard. The new commander's first intention was to re-occupy the old British cantonment outside Delhi and, if possible, to entrench his force on the dominant Ridge feature. This could not be done before the Pandis had been first driven from the Badli-ki-Serai, a large group of buildings standing five miles north of the city and overlooking the main road. After a furious and bloody battle, with heavy losses on both sides, the British took this place and then stormed on to sieze the Ridge. At the end of a long and exhausting day, the men of the Delhi Field Force stood on the crest of the long low hill and looked south towards the distant towers and minarets of the city.

Philip was again able to distinguish himself during the advance to the Ridge when he carried out a daring one-man reconnaissance ahead of the main force. A gunner officer, Henry Norman, later recalled the episode in his memoirs:

> 'Barnard's Column had halted for a short space after the victory of Badli-ki-Serai, at the point where the main road leading to Delhi, through the Sabzi Mand, was met by the road to the cantonment lying under the rocky Ridge.
>
> About a mile distant was the Najafgarh Canal, crossed by a bridge. It was evident that any attempt to cross the canal would be met by artillery fire. Accordingly, Salkeld, one of the Engineers, was despatched to inspect the bridge over the canal. He was at once greeted with a discharge from the guns on the Ridge, but returned to report that the bridge was only partly destroyed and that Barnard's guns could just get over.
>
> So we advanced, and in a short time were under a not very effective

artillery fire. Part of the side of the bridge had been broken away, and there were not six inches to spare when the gun wheels went over. A cannon shot struck the one remaining brick wall of the bridge as one of the guns passed it. Once over, the guns and skirmishers pushed smartly on and, reaching a low part of the Ridge to the right of the enemy's guns, wheeled to the right and at once silenced them.'

All day Philip Salkeld had been in the thick of the fight and was as tired as any of his fellows, but his labours were only just beginning. The following account makes plain the startling transition from his former duties with the Public Works Department:

> 'It was determined by the Chief Engineer in communication with the Brigadier commanding the Artillery to commence, on the night of June 8 and 9, two batteries in the neighbourhood of Hindoo Rao's House for two guns each. They were designated Salkeld's and Wilson's batteries. The armament of each was an 18-pounder and an 8-inch howitzer, and they were intended to subdue the fire of the enemy's guns in the Moree and Cashmere Bastion. An additional gun was subsequently added to Salkeld's battery, and on June 11 the whole of the guns aided by the mortars opened fire.
>
> On the night of June 15 and 16 a trench of communication was made between Salkeld's and Wilson's batteries, revetted inside with stones; the soil being very rocky the work was one of great difficulty, and proceeded slowly. The enemy was very quiet all night and day, and no attack was made on the position. On June 22 a party of Sappers under Lieutenant Salkeld destroyed the bridge carrying the Grand Trunk Road across the Nujufgurh Jheel drain. The bridge was of native construction, and of very massive proportions, having two arches and a central pier. A charge of 325 lb of powder, lodged in three chambers in the pier, effected complete demolition, destroying both arches.
>
> On the afternoon of August 26 the rebels attacked our right, bringing up six guns. Apparently they supposed that the main body of our troops had gone out with Nicholson's columns. About fifty sowars rashly charged up to within fifty yards of Salkeld's battery, where many paid the penalty of their rashness with their lives. Our casualties were twelve in this affair. General Nicholson's column returned at dusk. During the whole period of the siege, Salkeld was always cheerful and in good spirits, and had always a kind and encouraging word for those under him. He was a man of very simple and unpretending tastes, and had a dislike of show or display of any kind.'

On Sunday, 5 July, the attacking force suffered another loss in leadership when General Barnard also died of cholera. Described as 'a brave old

man who never spared himself when duty called', Barnard had arrived in India only a few months earlier. Apart from service in the Crimea, his career had not prepared him for the appalling strains imposed by the Mutiny. Debilitated by the harsh climate, he was vulnerable to India's many diseases. He was dead within six hours of the appearance of the first symptoms.

Barnard's successor was Major General Thomas Reed, another elderly officer, a veteran of Waterloo, who was so affected by the heat and by illness that he could take little active part. Seven days later he decided that he could not continue and retired to the hills. He was succeeded, briefly, by Brigadier General Neville Chamberlain, but he was badly wounded on 14 July. There was some discussion as to who should now take the senior post. It was agreed that Archdale Wilson had done well at the Hindun and had handled his men ably at the Badli-ki-Serai battle. He assumed the role of General Officer Commanding the Delhi Field Force. This decision so upset Colonel G Congreve, a senior officer who felt that the post should rightfully have gone to him, that he registered a protest and then went home to Simla.

It was a time of confusion and uncertainty in the senior ranks. The junior officers and other ranks were disconcerted to find that some of their leaders were quarrelsome old men, long past their prime both physically and mentally, and it would not have been surprising if the nerve of the youngsters had been shaken. It is to their eternal credit that they did not lose their resolve, nor did they lose control of the native troops who constituted a large part of the force.

The final days before the assault: exhausted gunners take a rest beside their 18-pounder cannon, ignoring the mortar shells lobbed at them from the city, and await the arrival of the 'bhisti' (water carrier) with his bulging goatskin. The weapon in the background is an 8-inch calibre howitzer. The scene is one of the emplacements on the forward slope of the Ridge, perhaps 'Salkeld's battery' or possibly 'Major Brind's battery'. (India Office Library & Records)

One of the most extraordinary young officers who distinguished themselves during this period was Lieutenant W S R Hodson of the 1st Bengal European Fusiliers. Later he would be remembered as 'Hodson of Hodson's Horse', but his main role with the Delhi Field Force was that of senior Intelligence Officer to first Anson and later Wilson. He had already made his mark in the Punjab campaign as a daring and courageous young man during the First and Second Sikh Wars whilst serving under Lumsden with the Guides. Now, in the long weeks of cut-and-thrust with the mutineers before the walls of Delhi, he made repeated reconnaissance missions into enemy territory. One of these was later described by a brother officer:

> 'As a scout Hodson's absolute contempt for anything like danger or even risk was simply unique, and of this we had a fair illustration only a few days after we had occupied our position in front of Delhi. There had been pretty heavy fighting in the Sabzi Mandi during the morning of the 12th June and when we got our orders for the attack, Hodson proposed to six or eight of us Engineers that we should go out and "take a look round" when towards sunset it became comparatively cool.
>
> According to appointment we went, most of us without arms and many without anything on our heads. Hodson led the way and, chatting merrily, took us straight into the Sabzi Mandi. As we went along the narrow street many of the enemy, with muskets and cross-belts, put their heads over parapets on the houses right and left and bobbed down again. Both Champain, who was to be my assistant Field Engineer in the coming attack, and Salkeld, looked glum as we advanced farther and farther, for neither had brought arms, and the former was glad indeed to get one of a brace of horse-pistols which constituted my armament.
>
> As we approached the Mori Bastion, Hodson's attention was drawn to an old woman crossing the road in front of him. With the sweetest of smiles he began questioning her about the various roads in that neighbourhood. At length one of the party suggested to Hodson that the place was hardly well chosen for a flirtation, whereupon we deliberately returned to camp by the same road and not a shot was fired at us the

whole evening. Salkeld, who won his V.C. and lost his life at the Kashmir Gate's final assault, told me that he regarded this reconnoitring trip as the maddest one he had ever made, but I am quite sure Hodson looked upon it as a most ordinary event.'

In the early hours of 14 September, Philip Salkeld was fetched from his tent to hear Duncan Home's orders for the attack planned for the morning. He was told that he would be Duncan's second-in-command and would take over the lead if Duncan fell. In the event, it was Duncan who survived without a scratch and Philip who was mortally wounded.

The muskets of that period discharged a lead ball nearly one ounce in weight. These weapons were cumbersome to handle and reload, but their 'stopping' power was formidable. The soft metal changed shape as it passed through a man's body, damaging internal organs and tearing large 'exit' wounds as the bullet emerged from the other side. Even when the wound itself was not mortal, the shock of the impact was enough to kill a man. Worse, in an age when battlefield surgery was still rudimentary, the jagged wounds were almost certain to become infected.

After being twice hit during the attack at the Kashmir Gate, Philip was taken to the field hospital and his smashed left arm amputated. His life hovered in the balance for many days. One of his visitors reported later, 'he was in agony', so it seems probable that he suffered a massive septicaemia. He was told of General Wilson's decision to reward him with the Victoria Cross, but he was visibly sinking. Wilson sent one of his aides, Lieutenant J R Turnbull of the 78th Regt (The Ross-shire Buffs), with a length of crimson ribbon which he pinned on Philip's bed-shirt. It was hoped that the gesture might stimulate him, but his only reaction was to say 'it will be gratifying to send it home.'

Philip Salkeld died on 10 October 1857, and his body was buried not far from the place where he was struck down. His name was later commemorated on the Calcutta memorial, and later still on the plaque fixed to the Kashmir Gate by Lord Napier.

The formal confirmation of his award of the Victoria Cross appeared in *The London Gazette* dated 18 June 1858 in a joint citation:

'Duncan Charles Home, Lieutenant: Philip Salkeld, Lieutenant, Bengal Engineers. Date of act of bravery: 14 Sept 1857. (Upon whom the Victoria Cross was provisionally conferred by Major General Sir Archdale Wilson, Bart, KCB). For their conspicuous bravery in the performance of the desperate duty of blowing in the Cashmere Gate of the Fortress of Delhi, in broad daylight, under a heavy fire of musketry, on the morning of 14 Sept 1857, preparatory to the assault. Would have been recommended to Her Majesty for confirmation in that distinction had they survived.'

Valhalla: the Nicholson Cemetery, Delhi, as it is today. Here Philip Salkeld and his friends still rest undisturbed, their graves almost hidden in the quiet groves of an area which has reverted to semi-jungle. This picture shows a corner of the cemetery two hundred yards west of the Kashmir Gate. A peaceful place, almost ghostly, it now lays isolated in the heart of India's busiest city. A project has been launched by the British Association for Cemeteries in South Asia to clear the scrub and to preserve as many of the memorials as can still be saved. (Photograph by kind permission of BACSA).

The ambiguous wording of this announcement might have left the reader wondering whether or not the authorities ever intended to issue the medals. Any doubts on this score were removed three weeks later when identical letters were despatched from the War Office to the fathers of the two dead officers (Major General Richard Home and the Reverend Robert Salkeld). This was the first occasion on which the decoration was presented to next-of-kin after the recipient's death. Both letters were dated 7 July 1858:

> 'I have received Her Majesty's Command to transmit to you herewith the decoration of the Victoria Cross which Maj Gen Sir Archdale

Wilson conferred in Her Majesty's name on your late lamented son to commemorate the daring act of gallantry which he performed on the memorable occasion of the assault on the stronghold of the Fortress of Delhi.

Her Majesty desires me to express to you the satisfaction which it would have afforded to Her to have confirmed the grant of this high distinction to this gallant soldier had it pleased Providence to have spared his life, and how gladly She would have presented to him this token of the sense which She entertains of his undaunted courage and conspicuous bravery. The Queen sincerely sympathises with you in his loss.

(signed) J. Peel'

When news of these events appeared in the English newspapers, popular response was one of compassion and pride. This was particularly the case in Dorset. Local editors made much of the story and the county gentry responded with a fund-raising campaign. One of the organisers, Mr S G Osborne, wrote an eloquent letter to the editor of *The Times*, explaining to the British public that money was required for the erection of a memorial at Fontmell Magna. Further, the HEIC was offering special cadetships to Philip's two younger brothers and cash was needed to pay the cost of their uniforms and kit. Mr Osborne also mentioned the important fact that Philip had been remitting funds back to his father from India to help the family finances. Indeed, Philip had saved the considerable sum of £1,000, which had been on deposit with the London & Delhi Bank (at Delhi) prior to the Mutiny, and this money was now lost. Mr Osborne concluded with the assurance that any surplus donations would be used to help one of Philip's sisters who, through lack of money, had been obliged to 'go into service' as a governess.

In the event, public response was so generous that the organisers decided in 1864 to use part of the fund for the public good. One and a half miles north of Sturminster Newton, on the road leading to Hazelbury Bryan and Dorchester, they erected a bridge over the River Divilish (a tributary of the Stour). Into each side of the bridge they set a stone block with the words 'Salkeld, Delhi, 1857'. Later, as the weight of vehicles increased, the local authority added a metal plaque with the non-committal warning 'to owners and drivers of traction engines – this bridge is insufficient to carry weights beyond the ordinary traffic of the district.'

The bridge is still in use and is known locally as 'the Salkeld bridge' but, of the hundreds of drivers who cross it every day, it is doubtful if more than a few are aware of its tragic origins.

The two brothers who benefitted from the public subscription were Charles Edward Salkeld and Richard Henry Salkeld. The former was

The memorial in the churchyard at Fontmell Magna in Dorset. One of the plaques on the plinth states: 'Sacred to the memory of Philip Salkeld, Lieutenant of Bengal Engineers, son of Revd Robt Salkeld & Elizabeth his wife of this Parish, born Octbr 13 1830 at Fontmell, died Octbr 11 1857 at Delhi, wounded mortally in blowing open the Cashmere Gate. Received on the battle field the Victoria Cross.' A second plaque states: 'In respect to his memory, in admiration of his worth and courage, a public subscription (begun in his own Parish) of more than eight hundred pounds was raised for the erection of this monument & for outfitting two younger brothers for military cadetships given by the Honble E I Company to mark their high sense of the character and service of Philip Salkeld.' (Photograph by kind permission Major Alan Harfield)

appointed Lieutenant in the Bengal Artillery from 8 June 1860, and Richard was appointed Ensign in the Bengal Infantry from 10 December 1859. Neither brother appears to have progressed beyond the rank of Lieutenant.

On 1 November 1858, to the background accompaniment of military reviews, firework displays and thanksgiving services, a Proclamation was formally read out at every cantonment in India. The document declared the abolition of John Company, the institution of direct rule by the British government, and an affirmation of the existing treaties with the independent principalities. It was a time of great change, a time to look to the future.

The embers of mutiny were not finally extinguished until 1859 but, as order and calm returned, so did the British start to analyse past mistakes, to record the events of the previous months and to erect memorials to those of their friends who had died. One such was a black marble tablet installed in the vestibule of St Paul's Cathedral, Calcutta. It listed the sixteen officers of the Bengal Engineers (including Philip Salkeld and Duncan Home) who fell during the Mutiny and was ornamented by the sculptor with a bas-relief of the scene at the Kashmir Gate on 14 September 1857.

It is reasonable to assume that the two younger Salkeld brothers, Charles and Richard, visited the Cathedral. It is even more probable that they followed the example of hundreds of other British officers who, over the years, made the pilgrimage to the Kashmir Gate and the Nicholson Cemetery. It must have been a solemn and awesome experience for them to see the place where Philip lost his life and earned his place in the VC roll of honour.

His Victoria Cross and his Mutiny medal have survived the passing years and are in the possession of a descendent member of the family in his home county.

APPENDIX G

John Smith VC

John Smith was every inch a tough professional soldier. When he won his Victoria Cross he was forty-three years of age, had already seen a great deal of hard campaigning in other wars, and had a full chest of medals to show for it. He was a calm steady man, supremely self-confident and a tower of strength to the two young officers whom he served at the Kashmir Gate.

He was born in February 1814, in Ticknall, a small village located in the extreme south of Derbyshire and seven miles east of Burton-upon-Trent. He was the son of Francis Smith, a cordwainer, and his wife Isabella. John was apparently the third of three sons, and sixth of eight children of the marriage.

When Francis and Isabella were married in Ticknall Church, in June 1798, they were both able to sign the register. Their witnesses, Thomas Jackson and Ann Wood, also both signed the register in person. This apparently trivial information provides the clue to John Smith's later military career; both of his parents, and his parents' friends, were respectable and literate. They raised their children according to the same standards.

In 1822 the family fell upon hard times. Isabella died prematurely and, with a business to manage and a large young family to care for, Francis was in difficulty. His brother, George, and his wife, moved down from Wirksworth, and they all lived and worked together. George also was a cordwainer, a broad description for any class of skilled independent artisan. Specifically, George was a maker of boots and shoes. When his nephew was old enough, he accepted the lad as an apprentice. John Smith completed his 'time' and spent his early years quietly in Ticknall, following his trade in the family business.

In October 1837, the spirit of adventure (or possibly a family dispute) drove him to leave the peace of the Trent Valley and 'go for a soldier'. He met a man named Hadnum, Recruiting Sergeant for the HEIC, who told of the fabulous life awaiting any fine young man prepared to seek his

fortune in the East Indies. John Smith followed the example of countless other country lads who had drunk ale with a Recruiting Sergeant; he accepted a token shilling and signed papers to be attested. He had just passed his twenty-third birthday. His papers show that he was above average height (five feet and eight inches), had grey eyes, sandy-coloured hair and a fresh complexion.

A few days later, on 30 October 1837, he arrived at the HEIC depôt at Chatham to start his eighteen months of basic and engineering training. On 27 March 1839, he embarked for India, sailing in the transport *Malcolm* and landing at Calcutta on 2 August. Sent initially to Roorkee, and then to Delhi, he soon made his mark and gained rapid promotion to the rank of Sergeant.

In November 1841, he joined the 5th Company and marched to Peshawar in the force commanded by Brigadier General Wild. A few weeks later, he and the 125 men of his company found themselves taking part in the First Afghan War when they advanced up the Khyber to Ali Musjid. A British army had been entirely destroyed by the Afghanis while attempting to withdraw from Cabul, and desperate attempts were being made to save the 13th Regt (Somerset Light Infantry) who were trapped in the fort at Jellalabad. The Afghanis were on the rampage and the border hill tribes held all the main vantage points along the British line of

The full-rigged ship 'Malcolm', in which John Smith made his one and only ocean voyage, depicted in Table Bay (Capetown) in 1839. Built on the Thames in 1826 and registered in London, she displaced 605 tons and was typical of the smaller cargo-cum-passenger ships which plied a regular trade between England and India. Part-owned by her skipper, Captain James Eyles, she was on regular charter to John Company and was a natural successor to the classic East Indiamen of the seventeenth and eighteenth centuries. (Oil painting by W J Huggins, National Maritime Museum)

advance. John Smith fought in various actions in the Shinwari country (at Mazina, Mamu-Khel, Jagdalak, Tezin and Haft Khotal) and subsequently took part in the re-occupation of Cabul.

At the end of the war he returned to Delhi and was transferred to the 7th Company. He did not take part in the Scinde or Gwalior campaigns of 1843, but served in the Sutlej campaign of 1845–6 and took part in the battle of Sobraon. Two years later he was again in action when, serving with the 3rd Company, he fought in the Punjab campaign. He was present at the siege and capture of Mooltan and at the battle of Goojerat. It will be recalled that Duncan Home joined the 3rd Company at this latter battle, so this was the first occasion when the two men met and worked together.

Following the final conquest of the Punjab and a cessation to the previous conflicts, the Sappers & Miners could turn their thoughts to more peaceful activities. In January 1851, John Smith was 'placed at the disposal of the Superintending Engineer of the Punjab circle for employment in the Department of Public Works'. His precise duties during the next three years are not known, but presumably he was engaged in various road construction projects.

On 12 January 1854, he was appointed Acting Assistant Overseer for the Meean Mir Division and was confirmed in this post when he passed his examinations two months later. For two or three years he was able to enjoy a stable domestic life with his wife and baby daughters in the family home at No 19, Artillery Lines, Meean Mir Cantonment, near Lahore. On 4 May 1844, at Amabala, he had married Mrs M A Styles (née Corrigean), the young widow of a trooper of the 12th Dragoons. Mortality amongst the soldiery was high, partly because there was a succession of wars and campaigns but mainly as the result of India's many unidentified diseases. White women were in short supply, hence it was customary for a widow to remarry quickly and to perhaps have several marriages, each of short duration. Smith was fortunate to find a wife and to enjoy twenty years in her company (interrupted only by the Second Sikh War and the Mutiny).

Everything went well until July 1856, when he is said to have 'incurred the displeasure of his superiors'. Reading between the lines, it seems likely that there may have been a clash of personalities with an officer of the Bengal Engineers. Smith came off badly from this affair. He was reduced to the ranks and, for some inexplicable reason, was posted as a gunner to the 3rd Company, 4th Battalion Bengal Artillery, then serving at Meean Mir. He protested through official channels and four months later was reinstated in the rank of Sergeant (without loss of seniority or pension rights) and was posted to the Bengal Sappers & Miners depôt at Roorkee.

The condition of the Bengal Sappers & Miners was at this time less than satisfactory. The total strength was sixteen British officers, twenty-three Indian officers, fifty British non-commissioned officers and privates, and 1,279 native other ranks. Many of the British officers were on secondment to Public Works Departments, but the bulk of the companies was concentrated at Roorkee. Peacetime economies had cut deeply into the equipment and administration of the Corps. Overall command had been assumed only eleven months earlier by Captain Edward Fraser, Bengal Engineers, an officer of considerable fighting experience but, with one exception, none of his junior officers had more than four years' service. None of them had been in action and many were still learning the languages and customs of the troops whom they commanded.

John Smith slotted himself comfortably into the quiet routine at Roorkee, tolerating the fresh-faced young subalterns so recently arrived from Chatham, and simply glad to be restored to his previous standing with his fellows. None of them noticed the symptoms of disaffection which were starting to appear in the ranks of the native sappers. All were blissfully unaware of the events which were coming to the boil at Meerut, sixty miles to the south.

On Sunday, 10 May 1857, the 3rd Light Cavalry rode to the Meerut local gaol, released 1,200 prisoners, were joined by two regiments of Bengal native infantry and, encouraged by the riff-raff of the local bazaar, started the appalling massacre which signalled the outbreak of the Great Mutiny. The majority of the Sappers & Miners serving there joined in the rebellion and followed the 3rd Light Cavalry and the other mutineers to Delhi. The surviving Europeans at Meerut sent out frantic warnings and appeals for aid to the surrounding cantonments. The survivors awaited the arrival of reinforcements and tried to fortify the cantonment in case the mutineers might return.

News of the disaster reached Roorkee early on 12 May. The senior instructor, Baird Smith, responded instantly by issuing orders for a relief force to be sent in boats down the Ganges Canal. Within six hours he had collected sufficient boats to carry several hundred loyal sappers and infantrymen, with their impedimenta, and they arrived at Meerut twenty-four hours later. They were commanded by Captain Fraser, and John Smith was part of the contingent.

The reception of Fraser's force, when they reached Meerut, was chilly. The British garrison troops and their officers were suspicious of the newcomers. They had already seen apparently friendly Indians turn in an instant into murderers of their own officers, and they now distrusted everything and everyone. The suspicion was so profound that it was decided to disarm the very troops who had come to aid the original garrison. The bewildered sappers were understandably resentful and they reacted by killing Captain Fraser. Many then fled and walked to Delhi where they joined the Pandi forces busily looting that city. Others went back quietly to Roorkee and reported for duty as though nothing had happened.

John Smith and the other British non-commissioned officers watched helplessly as their native rankers disappeared into the countryside. The loyal sappers who remained at Meerut consisted of five Indian officers and 124 Indian other ranks. Apart from Smith, there were forty-four British non-commissioned officers and privates. Among the latter group was No 400 Private Frank Burgess (alias Joshua Burgess Grierson), Bengal Sappers & Miners, who had arrived in India only five months before. Burgess was one of the men whom Smith subsequently recommended for inclusion in the 'explosion party' to attack the Kashmir Gate.

John Smith and his friends remained at Meerut for two more weeks, strengthening the defences and keeping careful watch for a possible attack. In the event, the cantonment remained quiet.

At sunset on 27 May, Archdale Wilson led his small column away from Meerut and headed towards Bhagput to join the Delhi Field Force. With him he had three men whose names would shortly become immortal: Salkeld, Smith and Burgess. The still-loyal sepoys of the Bengal Sappers & Miners had been issued with sidearms and ammunition, and were determined to salve the honour of their Corps. A small detachment was left behind to look after the sick and to guard the heavy equipment.

John Smith took part in the battle of the Hindun bridge and the assault at Badli-ki-Serai. He came through these actions, and the seizing of the Ridge, without injury. During the following weeks his 'old campaigner' experience helped him to avoid the diseases which struck down so many of his friends (at one stage fully half of the 5,000 men of Wilson's force were in hospital and, of these, 1,100 were Europeans). Then came the night of 13 September and Smith was detailed to act as third-in-command of the 'explosion party'. His selection can be attributed to his known fighting record and the fact that both Home and Salkeld had seen him in action.

John Smith was one of the only two Europeans to survive the attack by more than a few weeks and he later wrote a lively eyewitness account:

'The party for blowing in the gate, the 60th Rifles leading, went off at the double from Ludlow Castle, until they arrived at the cross-roads leading to the Customs, and they opened out right and left, the Sappers going to the gate led by Lieut Home and one bugler (Hawthorne), Lieut Salkeld with the party carrying the powder a few paces behind, three European non-commissioned officers, and nine natives with twelve bags of twenty-five pounds each. My duty was to bring up the rear, and see that none of them remained behind. Lieut Salkeld had passed through the temporary (outer) gate with Sergts Carmichael and Burgess, but four of the natives had stopped behind the above gate and refused to go on. I had to put down my bag and take my gun, and threatened to shoot them, when Lieut Salkeld came running back, and said, "Why the hell don't you come on?" I told him that there were four men behind the gate, and that I was going to shoot them. He said, "Shoot them, damn their eyes, shoot them!" I said, "You hear the orders, and I will shoot you," raising the gun slowly to the 'present' to give fair time, when two men went on. Lieut Salkeld said, "Do not shoot; with your own bag it will be enough." I went on, and only Lieut Salkeld and Sergt Burgess were there; Lieut Home and the bugler had jumped into the ditch, and Sergt Carmichael was killed as he went up with his powder on his shoulder, evidently having been shot from the wicket while crossing the broken part of the bridge along one of the beams. I placed my bag, and then, at great risk, reached Carmichael's bag from in front of the wicket, placed it, arranged the fuse for the explosion and reported all ready to Lieut Salkeld, who held the slow match (not a port-fire, as I have seen stated). In stooping down to light the quick match, he put out his foot, and was shot through the thigh from the wicket, and in falling had the presence of mind to hold out the slow match, and told me to fire the charge. Burgess was next to him and took it. I told him to fire the charge and keep cool. He turned round and said, "It won't go off, sir; it has gone out, sir" (not knowing that one officer had fallen into the ditch). I gave him a box of lucifers, and as he took them, he let them fall into my hand, he being shot through the

The portico at the Kashmir Gate where Duncan Home's 'explosion party' made its attack. The entrance was closed by two inward-opening heavy timber doors mounted on pairs of thick iron hinges. Set into the right-hand door was a small wicket gate so that one person at a time could pass in or out of the city, without the need to open the main door. The depth of the brick overhang enabled Sergeant Smith to crouch down close to the left-hand door, trying to light the fuse, without being hit by marksmen shooting through the wicket or downwards from the parapet. (Photographed in 1977 by Mrs J Harfield)

body at the wicket also, and fell over after Lieut Salkeld. I was then left alone, and keeping close to the charge, seeing from where the others were shot, I struck a light, when the port-fire in my fuse went off in my face, the light not having gone out as we thought. I took up my gun and jumped into the ditch, but before I had reached the ground the charge went off, and filled the ditch with smoke so that I saw no one. I turned while in the act of jumping, so that my back would come to the wall to save me from falling. I stuck close to the wall, and by that I escaped being smashed to pieces, only getting a severe bruise on the leg, the leather helmet saving my head. I put my hands along the wall and touched someone, and asked who it was. "Lieut Home," was the answer. I said, "Has God spared you? Are you hurt?" He said, "No," and asked the same from me. As soon as the dust cleared a little, we saw Lieut Salkeld and Burgess covered with dust; their lying in the middle of the ditch had saved them from being smashed to pieces and covered by the debris from the top of the wall, the shock only toppling the stones over, which fell between where we stood and where they lay. I went to Lieut Salkeld and called the bugler to help me to remove him under the bridge as the fire had covered upon us, and Lieut Salkeld's arm was broken. Lieut Salkeld would not let us remove him, so I put a bag of powder under his arm for a pillow, and with the bugler's puggery bound up his arms and thigh, and I left the bugler to look to him, and went to Burgess, took off his sword, which I put on, and did what I could for him. I got some brandy from Lieut Home, and gave to both, also to a Havildar (Tilok Singh), who had his thigh shot through, and was under the bridge by a ladder which had been put into the ditch by mistake by the Rifles. I then went to the rear for three stretchers and brought them, one of which was taken from me by an officer of the Rifles. I had to draw my sword and threaten to run anyone through who took the other two. I put them into the ditch, and with the bugler's assistance got Lieut Salkeld into one, and sent him with him, charging him strictly not to leave him until he had placed him in the hands of a surgeon, and with the assistance of a Naick who had come to the Havildar, got Burgess into one, and sent the Havildar and the Naick with him, I being scarcely able to walk, and in a few minutes he returned to say that he was dead, and asked for further orders. I told him to take him to the hospital. After assisting to clear away the gate and make the roadway again, I went on to the front to see what was going on.'

Smith's precise movements during the following days are not known. It seems likely that he was employed in the supervision of various engineering tasks during the battle to clear the city of mutineers (two-thirds of the Bengal Engineer officers having been killed or wounded before and during the assault). After the recapture of the city, those engineers and sappers who were still on their feet were employed for a time at Delhi, repairing the damaged fortifications and disposing of dangerous ordnance. The battered walls around the Kashmir Gate were left untouched as a memorial to the assault. Subsequently the engineers and sappers were attached to various columns operating throughout Oudh, restoring order and executing (often with great brutality) any known Pandis who fell into their hands. Some of the sappers took part in the operations for the relief of Lucknow, but Smith was not one of these.

He was attached to the flying column led by Brigadier General George Barker, RA, and was involved in punitive operations for the next eighteen months. There were many skirmishes with Pandi troops during this time, and two full-pitched battles. The first of these was the clash at Sandela, on 7 October 1858, and three days later there was the bloody encounter when Barker's men stormed and captured the fort at Birwah (for which Barker subsequently received the KCB). John Smith, by now wearing the distinctive piece of crimson ribbon upon his breast, took part in all these operations.

His award of the Victoria Cross appeared in *The London Gazette* dated 27 April 1858, the same edition in which Bugler Hawthorne's award was announced. These announcements pre-dated the announcements for Home and Salkeld by several weeks, the delay resulting from the circumstances already described in Appendix A (the story of the so-called 'posthumous awards'):

> 'John Smith, Sergt, Bengal Sappers & Miners. Date of act of bravery: 14 Sept 1857. For conspicuous gallantry, in conjunction with Lieuts Home and Salkeld; in the performance of the desperate duty of blowing in the Cashmere Gate of the Fortress of Delhi in broad daylight, under a heavy and destructive fire of musketry, on the morning of 14 Sept 1857, preparatory to the assault. (General Order of Major General Sir Archdale Wilson, Bart, KCB, dated headquarters, Delhi City, 21st Sept 1857).'

The Mutiny ended, he returned in July 1859 to his family at Jullundur and was appointed local Sub-Conductor and Barrack Master. On 17 March of the following year he received his commission as Ensign, Bengal Engineers, and then moved to Peshawar as 1st Class Barrack Master in February 1862. At the end of that year he was given responsibility for the barracks at Sudathu Dagshai and Kasauli. Similar posts followed when he was posted to Darjeeling (January 1864) and then to Ambala (March 1864). He was now fifty years of age, had obtained pleasant and interesting employment, and could look forward to taking his pension in the near future. He owned property (two bungalows at Meean Mir), and he had the substantial sum of 5,000 rupees in the bank. He could afford to educate his four daughters (Isobel, Eliza, Emily and Frances) at the convent school at Mussoorie, a popular hill station and sanatorium in the Himalayan foothills. Fate had been kind to him and he could look back with satisfaction over a long career which had commenced with a simple country lad leaving his cobbler's bench in Derbyshire.

Sadly, fate had one last trick to play on the heroes of the Kashmir Gate. On 26 June 1864, John Smith developed dysentery while on leave at Jullundur with his family. The attack was violent and within hours he was dead from exhaustion.

Next day he was buried with full military honours in the Artillery Cemetery. He left his property and other possessions to his widow, Mary Ann, making particular mention that she should receive his medals and his three horses and his pony. It was a poignant end for a man who had seen so much fighting and who had never suffered any hurt worse than a bruised leg.

APPENDIX H

Robert Hawthorne VC

In common with many other famous fighting regiments, the Oxfordshire Light Infantry had a long and varied history. First raised in 1755 as the 54th Regiment of Foot, it had been subsequently re-numbered the 52nd. Under the influence of its brilliant Colonel-Commandant, Sir John Moore, it evolved into a *corps d'élite* of specially selected troops – highly trained, fast and hard-hitting. In the early decades of its existence, the regiment fought with distinction in the North Americas under Wolfe, in India under Cornwallis, in the Peninsula under Wellington, and again under the Iron Duke at Waterloo.

After the final defeat of Napoleon, in 1815, the regiment entered the long hiatus of the Forty Years' Peace. There followed many years of routine garrison duties in Canada, the West Indies, England and Ireland before, in 1853, the regiment made the long passage out to India. They were returning to the land where their grandfathers had fought with distinction in the Mysore campaigns.

The four years preceding the Mutiny were served in Oudh, in the Punjab and on the border with Afghanistan, helping to hold the territory annexed by the British after the Second Sikh War. When the first rumblings of the impending storm were detected – in March 1857 – the regiment was stationed at Sialkot, 70 miles north of Lahore and 300 miles north-east from Delhi. The senior British commanders in north-west India – John Lawrence, Nicholson, Chamberlain, and other equally experienced campaigners – were deeply worried by what they heard and saw. A moveable column, commanded by John Nicholson and including the 52nd Regiment, was formed. Its purpose was to support the measures being taken to disarm and disband native regiments known to be disaffected. On 25 May the 52nd left their sick and followers at Sialkot and took to the road.

Throughout the following weeks the regiment was constantly on the move and soon in action with rebel troops in various parts of the Punjab. It was the hottest time of the year and several men died of heat stroke.

Despite the baking heat and choking dust-storms, the troops revelled in the type of warfare for which they were specifically trained: long forced marches and sharp fire-fights. On 12 July, for example, they covered 40 miles in less than twenty hours and shortly afterwards went into battle at Trimmooghat against a mutineer force three times stronger than themselves. Armed with the new Enfield rifle – 'the very king of weapons' – the regiment was in action for the first time in forty-two years and, as though to mark the change in their fortunes, they fought in light-weight khaki cotton drill (having abandoned their traditional 'rifle green' at Sialkot).

By early August the worst outbreaks of mutiny in the Punjab had been contained. The situation was still dangerous, but it was agreed that the recapture of Delhi must take priority over all other operations. The time had come for the big gamble – to withdraw troops and guns from the Punjab and send them down the Grand Trunk Road for the main trial of strength with the Pandi leaders.

The 52nd (Oxfordshire Light Infantry) Regiment joined Archdale Wilson's force on the Ridge, north of Delhi, on 14 August. They marched into camp 680 strong, with only sixteen sick. Within four weeks their effective strength had been whittled down by battle losses and sickness to 240 all ranks. One of the men still fit for duty was a burly, bearded Irishman by the name of Robert Hawthorne.

Robert was born in 1822 in Maghera, a large village midway along the road from Londonderry to Belfast. His family was poor and his schooling was sketchy, but he learned to write his own name and was probably semi-literate and numerate when he left school, at around the age of ten, to start work as a labourer. He must have been physically well-developed because, at the age of 14, he was able to enlist in the 52nd Regiment for boy service. The Recruiting Sergeant took the lad to Athlone, in the County of Roscommon, where he was attested before a Magistrate, 'for unlimited service', on 15 February 1836.

Sent to the depôt in England, he was given the regimental number 945, kitted out, and put through his paces on the basic training course. It seems probable that he also received some musical training with a view to becoming a drummer or bugler. His papers show that he was fair-skinned, had brown hair and light grey eyes. We do not know his height at that time but, with good food and plenty of exercise, he had attained five feet and eight inches by the time he was ready for overseas service.

Robert served briefly in Barbados (surviving the various fevers which struck down so many of his comrades in the West Indies) before moving on to St John's, Quebec Province, and to Fredericton, New Brunswick. Returning to England, the regiment was split into company detachments in Cheshire and Lancashire, giving aid to the civil authorities during the unrest following the emergence of the 'Chartist' movement in 1849.

Then, in 1851, came the next move, this time to Ireland where there were still Government anxieties in the wake of the attempted 'Young Ireland' rebellion of 1848. The regiment served for nearly two years in Limerick before making, in the spring of 1853, the long voyage to the land where Robert Hawthorne was destined to find his moment of glory.

Throughout all these years he followed a career illuminated by only two recorded events. In 1844, at the age of 22, he was 'appointed' to the post of Bugler. His substantive rank remained that of Private, but the appointment was significant in terms of prestige and additional pay. The regimental buglers spent much of their time in the vicinity of the Orderly Room and in the presence of officers. Consequently, apart from being trusted to sound the correct calls at the appointed hours during the working day, they were also expected to be unusually discreet and smart in appearance.

Further, it was the buglers who, under the supervision of the Colour Sergeant, had charge of the arrangements for administering the lash. British soldiers were liable to be condemned to this form of corporal punishment for a number of different offences and, although it was in some regiments applied only rarely, it was not totally abolished until 1867. Robert Hawthorne was a powerfully built man and this attribute made him ideal for wielding the whip. A macabre aspect of the selection process for aspiring buglers was the preference for a proportion of left-handed men. With two buglers delivering the blows, a thorough scourging of the victim's back was ensured – half the blows being laid across from one direction, half from the other.

The second event recorded in his papers was, ironically, his own Regimental Court Martial. On 27 June 1850, while the regiment was stationed in Liverpool, he was arrested for what must have been a relatively serious offence. He spent nineteen days under guard in hospital and was then tried on 18 July. The sentence of the Court was a total of forty-eight days' confinement and the loss of one penny per day of his pay for the following six months. We are not told the nature of the charge which led to this fall from grace, but the facts suggest that Robert's fighting Irish blood had involved him in a brawl. What is so surprising is that he had previously served more than fourteen years with the regiment – 'man and boy' – without a stain upon his character. Clearly there must have been some exceptional circumstances surrounding this unfortunate episode.

Robert's part in the assault on the Kashmir Gate, and the brave conduct which led to his immediate award of the Victoria Cross, have been already described in the preceding pages. The announcement of his award, together with those of Duncan Home, Philip Salkeld and John Smith, appeared in the Field Force Orders dated 21 September (which also included the award of a fifth VC, to 2764 Lance Corporal Henry Smith of the 52nd Regiment, who had rescued a wounded comrade under heavy fire during the first day's street fighting):

> 'Bugler Robert Hawthorn, Her Majesty's 52nd Regiment, who accompanied the explosion party, and not only most bravely performed the dangerous duty on which he was employed, but previously attached himself to Lieut Salkeld, of the Engineers, when dangerously wounded, bound up his wounds under a heavy musketry fire, and had him removed without further injury.'

Seven months later, very similar wording appeared in *The London Gazette* dated 27 April 1858 (coupled with the announcement of John Smith's award). There are two points to be noted. First, the bugler's name appears in some accounts as Hawthorn, in others as Hawthorne. Reference to his army record of service and to his Death Certificate confirms the latter as the correct spelling. Secondly, Robert's citation suggests that it was he who was instrumental in trying to save Salkeld's life. This is at variance with John Smith's own eyewitness account. Perhaps they shared the task of giving first aid; we shall never know the precise truth and, in the final analysis, it did not really matter. Philip Salkeld was in any event a doomed man.

Robert fought alongside the dwindling survivors of his regiment during the battle to re-occupy Delhi. By 20 September the last of the Pandis were either dead or had made their escape to join mutinous troops in other towns and cities. A year and a half more were to pass before they were all finally killed, captured or dispersed.

The 52nd took no part in these later operations. They stayed at Delhi for a while, billeted in the Main Magazine building, a mile or so north of the city. Robert Hawthorne's precise duties during this period are not recorded, but there is a note that he and another bugler of the 52nd, Michael Johnson, were given permission to accompany a group of Sikh irregular cavalry and to visit the grave of Brigadier General John Nicholson. Robert had never had direct contact with the legendary Nicholson, but the reputation of the man was such that many common soldiers, both British and Indian, Robert included, felt compelled to pay their last respects at the graveside.

Archdale Wilson was splitting his force into a number of flying columns so that he could clear the surrounding area and send reinforcements to assist in raising the siege at Lucknow. The 52nd asked if they might join Sir John Hope Grant's column, then being formed, and to march down country to this latter city. However, with only eleven officers, two surgeons and 160 rank and file still able to march, it was obvious that they could take no useful part in further operations and were ordered back to

The gravestone of Brigadier General John Nicholson shortly after its completion. Several hundred men of the Delhi Field Force found their final resting place in both this cemetery and the Rajpur cemetery a short distance to the rear. Some of the graves were distinguished by ornate headstones, but many of the dead were buried in haste, without markers, singly or in mass graves, and could not be subsequently recorded. The archives do not reveal the location of the graves of the three Europeans who failed to survive the Kashmir Gate affair - Salkeld, Carmichael and Burgess. (India Office Library & Records)

the Punjab. One of their junior officers, Reginald Wilberforce, recorded the sad journey:

> 'This return to the Punjab was perhaps the hardest task that year. The excitement was all over; there was nothing to be looked forward to, the long night hours of the regular march were never enlivened with a song - even the well-known "Jolly Shilling" was never heard. No band to play us out of camp, no bugle-band to take up the music - in fact our bugle-band was a thing of the past, and it was two years before we had the bugles to play at mess again. The men were jaded and weary, they dragged along the road, and we all felt a sense of relief when on the 1st November we marched into Jullunder, where we remained until next year, when we got back to Sealkote.'

Although left out of the great battles which followed the taking of Delhi, the men of the 52nd did at least have the consolation of six months' bonus pay for their part in that victory. In addition, they each received from the Prize Agents their official share of the wealth looted from the desolated city. And, unofficially, some of them returned to the Punjab with their packs well laden with specie and valuable artefacts which they had encountered while fighting their way through the city.

The regiment returned to England in June 1859. Robert Hawthorne preceded them by some months, having been sent back with a draft of 'time expired' men and invalids. The last two years of his army life were served at the regimental depôt at Chatham and then, on 20 April 1861, he was granted his discharge 'as an indulgence at his own request, free with pension, after 21 years' service' (to which must be added four years' boy service).

He had been granted four Good Conduct badges during the final years of his career, but the earlier blot on his record – the Court Martial – told against him when he was considered for the award of a Long Service and Good Conduct medal. It was decided that he was not eligible. This is strange, because such awards were, to a certain degree, within the discretion of the Commanding Officer of each regiment. Given the fact that Robert was a VC winner, and allowing for only one recorded crime in 25 years, it would have been an act of grace to have granted a third medal to adorn the hero's jacket.

Robert Hawthorne, now 39 years of age, retired to Manchester and stayed there for the remainder of his life. He married a lady named Christina Adelaide Neale and they lived initially at Malden Lane. Later, as the family grew, they moved to 1 Huntingdon Street, off Tuer Street, in the tough working-class area of Chorlton-on-Medlock, near the city centre. There were five children by the marriage – Robert, Charles Kenrick, Jane Neale, Lily Maud and Jessie – but neither of the boys followed their father's example by joining the Oxfordshire Light Infantry.

Robert took employment as a porter with a local financial institution known as 'the Old Bank', a title reflecting the fact that it was established in 1819 and was therefore one of the earliest private banks in Manchester. The founders were Cunliffe, Brooks & Company. The two families intermarried and, at the time when Robert Hawthorne worked there, the

Robert Hawthorne VC, late of the 52nd Regiment, photographed shortly after his retirement from the army in 1861 and proudly displaying his two awards (the VC and the Mutiny medal with the single clasp 'Delhi'). By leaving unfastened several top buttons on his waistcoat he was following the contemporary fashion. (Photograph by kind permission of the Royal Greenjackets Museum, Winchester)

owner was Sir William Cunliffe-Brooks JP. He was reputed to be 'the richest person in England outside the Royal family,' and he personally selected (and took a close interest in) each and every one of his employees. The bank remained in family hands until 1901 when it was acquired by Lloyd's Bank Limited. No doubt Robert's VC was an advantage to him in securing a post with such an excellent employer.

It is a moving testimonial to the remarkable *esprit de corps* of the old Oxfordshire Light Infantry that the Hawthorne family was frequently visited by officers of the regiment who ensured that all was well. The last of Robert's sons, Charles, died in 1943, and the last of his daughters, Mrs Adie, in 1951. She was visited regularly right up until the time of her death, nearly a century after her father won his VC and seventy-two years after the old soldier himself had died! One of the visiting officers was Colonel Richard Crosse, a descendant of Captain Charles Crosse, the first British officer to enter Delhi through the shattered Kashmir Gate on 14 September 1857.

Robert died at his home in Huntingdon Street on 2 February 1879 at the comparatively young age of fifty-seven. The cause of his death was rheumatic fever. On the following day his widow purchased a grave at the nearby Ardwick Cemetery and made arrangements for a private funeral. She also received a visitor in her front parlour, a reporter from a local newspaper which wished to print a short announcement of the VC hero's premature death.

The newspaper report was seen by a detached officer of the 52nd, Major the Honourable A E Dalzell (later Brigadier General the Right Honourable Earl Carnwath CB), at the time employed as Superintendent of Gymnasia, Northern District. He decided instantly that Robert should be accorded a full military funeral. He travelled to Manchester, obtained the agreement of the widow and contacted the nearest military unit, the 96th Regiment of Foot, then stationed at Salford Barracks. Their commanding officer agreed to provide an officer, a party of soldiers to fire three volleys over the grave, and a bugler to sound Last Post (a duty which Robert himself had many times performed).

Lack of time prevented any other representatives of his regiment attending the ceremony, but Major Dalzell and his batman, Private Hilyer, followed the solemn procession to Ardwick Cemetery where, as the officer reported later, 'we two 52nd men were the last who looked upon his resting place'.

A curious feature of Robert's gravestone is the inscription which states that his age, at the time of his death, was fifty-two. This is incorrect. The official records show that he was fifty-seven. Perhaps, having decided to marry at a relatively late stage in life (when he was approximately forty), he indulged in a gentle deception by telling his bride-to-be that he was five years younger than his true age. Christina produced five children and lived until 1909, so presumably she was significantly younger than Robert.

Christina kept Robert's VC, and his Mutiny medal with clasp 'Delhi', for several years, but they then passed into the private collection of Mr J B Gaskell. Subsequently, on 19 February 1909, they were offered at auction by Messrs Glendinning and were purchased, for the sum of £108.00, by the officers of the Oxfordshire & Buckinghamshire Light Infantry. They are now on display at the Royal Greenjackets Museum, Winchester.

Robert's courage at the Kashmir Gate was marked in one particularly unusual manner. Soon after the battle a soldier of 'C' Company composed some verses which were adopted as a marching song by the regiment. On the 50th anniversary of the battle, 14 September 1907, they were sung again by 2952 Private William McKenna, late of the 52nd, at a smoking Concert given by the Sergeants' Mess. History does not tell us the tune to which these stirring lines were sung:

Come fill, fill up a bumper,
Our toil at length is done,
Since the Pandies are defeated,
And Delhi has been won.
Great men they were in their own eyes,
At least then so they thought,
So we took the shine out of them,
On the 12th, at Trimmooghat.
Chorus
When a-hunting we did go, my boys,
A-hunting we did go,
To chase the Pandies, night and day,
And levelled Delhi low.

A-thirsting to avenge, my boys,
The bloodshed that was done
On poor defenceless women,
'Ere Delhi had been won,
We made the Pandies for to know,
And caused them for to feel
That British wrongs should be avenged,
By sterling British steel.
Chorus

The advance through the Kashmir Gate by Colonel Campbell's column – one of the many artistic impressions subsequently published in England. The storming party of the 52nd Regiment crosses the bridge and enters the city while (on the skyline) the green-jacketed skirmishers of the 60th Rifles await their turn. (Print from regimental records)

On the 14th of September,
  I remember well the date,
We showed the Pandies a new hit,
  When we stormed the Cashmere Gate;
Their grape-shot, shell, and musketry,
  They found but little good,
When British soldiers were outside,
  A-thirsting for their blood.
Chorus

To Hawthorne, too, three cheers are due;
  The "Advance" he three times sounded,
And attended on Lieutenant Salkeld,
  When dangerously wounded.
Regardless of all danger,
  'Ere the Cashmere Gate was won,
He upheld the Fifty-Second,
  And his duty nobly done.
Chorus

Several officers of the 52nd Regt later jotted down their recollections of those phrenetic days of close-quarter battle. A typical account was that composed by young Ensign Wingfield in a letter written on 26 September 1857, to his father in England:

> 'You will have seen, by the telegraph, before this reaches you, that Delhi has at last been taken. I can only write a few lines to say that I am quite well. I escaped without a scratch, thank God! We stormed the walls on the 14th of this month. Owing to the failure of the attacks of two of the columns, we did not take the whole of the city the first day, but, having advanced steadily from street to street, with some hard fighting, on the 20th the whole of the walls were ours, and the enemy bolted – when they found that they could hold it no longer. They fought desperately and in great numbers, but who could stand before the persistent bravery of the British soldier? Our loss was: sixty-two officers and 1,100 men killed and wounded. The 52nd lost one officer killed and three wounded, and over ninety men killed and wounded, out of 250 that went into action. Poor Bradshaw was the officer killed; he joined with me. He was a fine,

brave young fellow, and was shot dead by my side, charging a gun that was firing grape at us down a street; another officer – Atkinson – was wounded at the same time. Captain Bayley was wounded in the arm while advancing on the Cashmere gate, and Colonel Campbell was wounded while charging up a street. I had a narrow escape of being cut down at one time, for I was skirmishing on the tops of houses, when the enemy's cavalry charged below and the Sikhs on our side got a panic and bolted; our men had to retreat, and when I looked down I saw them retiring firing, the Sikhs cutting and the cavalry charging us. I was cut off, so I thought it best to make a rush for it. I called the men with me to follow me, and we ran down into the street, when the sowars saw me; three of them surrounded me and cut at me with their tulwars, but not having a revolver with which to defend myself, I dodged under their horses and cut in behind our men, who had by this time formed up and were firing slap in my face. How I escaped being shot by our own men I cannot conceive. We did not kill as many of the enemy as we expected, as they had the advantage of us, behind walls, but whenever we caught them in the open we shot and bayonetted them to a man, no quarter being given.

The Palace was taken on the 20th, without resistance, though had they remained in it and fought well, I don't think we could have taken it for a long time and not without great loss to us; but they had nearly all fled, having taken the king and the princes with them. The king was taken next day a few miles from the city; the princes were shot on the spot, and their bodies were lying until yesterday exposed to the public gaze in the main street. The treasure and plunder of all descriptions is being sold every day by auction; the proceeds will, I expect, be immense. Three of our regiments have marched down country to open the road to Cawnpore; I do not yet know whether we remain here or go up country; they must leave some regiments here to garrison the city. We are at present quartered in the magazine, and are pretty comfortable; the health of the men is improving.'

One man whose health was less than good was Sergeant Major James Streets, the senior non-commissioned officer of the 52nd Regiment. Although only thirty-nine years of age, this grizzled veteran had already earned his Long Service & Good Conduct medal, five months before the assault on Delhi. Following the demolition of the Kashmir Gate, he was one of the front-runners through the portico and up along the city wall to sieze the ramparts of the Water Bastion. The mutineer gunners manning this strong-point resisted fiercely but, with boots, fists and the bayonet, the light infantrymen cleared the enemy from the bastion and from the surrounding houses.

James Streets inspired the younger soldiers throughout this short and bloody engagement. His bravery made him an obvious candidate for the Victoria Cross. At this point, however, he was shot down by a Pandi musketeer. The ball passed through Streets' abdomen, emerging from the other side of his body. Miraculously, he survived the attentions of the surgeons and, after three months in hospital, was able to rejoin his regiment at Jullundur in December.

He was marked out for special reward but, instead of receiving the covetted Cross, he was granted an Ensignancy in the 75th Regiment of Foot. In January 1858 he joined his new regiment and served with them for two years before being forced into half-pay retirement as a result of poor health caused by his wound and by sunstroke.

Leaving their adult daughter in India, he and his wife retired to England and finally settled in Ilminster in the county of Somerset. His half-pay permitted them to live a life of reasonable comfort, but his health declined steadily and he developed a form of cerebral palsy. In April 1883, increasingly depressed by his own condition and only sixty-five years of age, James Streets committed suicide by slashing his throat with a kitchen knife. Another of the forgotten heroes of the Kashmir Gate assault, he was one more of its victims.

APPENDIX I

The Forgotten Men

Only the chance cruelties of war prevented two other members of Duncan Home's party from receiving the supreme award for valour, the Victoria Cross. Their names were Carmichael and Grierson, and no account of the action at the Kashmir Gate is complete without reference to them.

ANDREW BLAIR CARMICHAEL was an Irishman. He was born in Dublin in 1827, in St Peter's Parish, and enjoyed a better-than-average education. On 10 September 1847, at the age of twenty, he enlisted in Dublin for service with the Honourable East India Company artillery. His civilian occupation was given as 'clerk' and this fact, combined with his city upbringing, suggests that he was of a higher intelligence than the majority of his contemporaries who escaped Ireland's grinding poverty by joining the armies of Great Britain and India.

He was immensely tall for that period, having a height of nearly six feet. His complexion was stated to be 'fresh', and he had brown hair and 'black' eyes. Shortly after enlistment he was transferred from the artillery training course and ear-marked for service with the Bengal Sappers & Miners.

He arrived at Chatham on 22 September 1847 and there completed nearly two years of training before sailing for India, in the transport *Ellenborough*, on 6 June 1849. He landed in India on 14 October and was posted to the Corps headquarters at Ludhiana, midway between Delhi and Lahore.

Two years later he was promoted First Corporal and selected as a probationary student at the Civil Engineering College, Roorkee. He studied there for a year, passed his examinations, and was posted as an Assistant Overseer in the Department of Public Works, Ambala Division. In December 1853 he transferred to a similar post at Meean Mir, near Lahore. One month later he was joined by John Smith, the man in whose company he was destined to die before the walls of Delhi. The two worked together until July 1854 when Andrew Carmichael 'was permitted to resign his appointment in the Public Works Department' before rejoining his Corps at Meerut.

There followed a short interlude while he worked on detachment with the Garrison Engineer at Lahore; he then returned to Meerut. Promoted to the rank of Sergeant, he was posted to Roorkee and was serving at this station when the Mutiny broke out in May 1857. He was one of the Bengal Sappers & Miners who were mobilised by Baird Smith and made the rapid passage down the Ganges Canal to reinforce the British survivors at Meerut.

Andrew subsequently took part in Archdale Wilson's march from Meerut to Delhi, being involved *en route* in the battles at the Hindun bridge, at Badli-ki-Serai, and for possession of the Ridge. He was one of the many non-commissioned officers who played a key role in the construction of the siege batteries during the long and desperate weeks leading up to the final assault. He was also one of the few who were not killed, injured or struck down by illness during this time.

The selection of Andrew Carmichael as a member of Duncan Home's team was based not only upon the fact that he was still physically capable of the effort involved, but also that he was unusually intelligent and well-trained. He was only thirty years of age when he died, so it is probable that he would have gone far in his profession had he lived.

The full circumstances of his death have been already described in the preceding pages. Briefly he was one of Duncan's 'carrying party' and was the third man to reach the broken bridge in front of the Kashmir Gate. As he ran onto the damaged timbers, so was the small wicket gate opened from the inside by several Pandi soldiers. They pointed their muskets through the gap, firing a point-blank volley at the attackers. One of these shots struck Andrew, killing him instantly. His bag of powder fell forward and landed on the planking immediately in front of the open wicket. It was from this exposed position that it was retrieved, a few moments later, by the intrepid John Smith (who then stacked it with the others against the stout wooden doors).

Andrew died intestate, a bachelor. At the time of his death his documents were not annotated with the names of any immediate next-of-kin and it is not known who eventually received his estate of 272 rupees (approximately £27.00 sterling).

JOSHUA BURGESS GRIERSON (alias FRANK BURGESS) was a Scot. He was born in St Cuthbert's Parish, Edinburgh, in 1835. After leaving school he took employment as a clerk. As in the case of Andrew Carmichael, his occupation and birthplace suggest that he was of higher intelligence and better education than most of his contemporaries.

It is impossible to know what motives caused him to enlist in the forces of the Honourable East India Company on 10 September 1854 at the age of nineteen. The fact that he enlisted under an assumed name suggests that he may have been anxious to cover his tracks from pursuing creditors or the irate father of a disappointed young lady. In any event, he went to Glasgow, signed his attestation papers on 9 November for 10 years' service with the HEIC European infantry (using the name Frank Burgess), and travelled south to England for his initial training.

His record shows that he was a slightly-built young man (he was five feet and five and a half inches in height), with a fresh complexion, grey eyes and fair hair. Shortly after reaching the HEIC depôt he was transferred to the Bengal Sappers & Miners (another indication of superior intellectual capability). He completed his two years' training and sailed, in the transport *Minden*, for India, where he landed on 29 November 1856. The first posting was Roorkee and he was still there when the Mutiny exploded five months later.

Joshua (alias Frank) was a member of the relief column which travelled by boat from Roorkee to Meerut, and later marched to Delhi. Like John Smith and Andrew Carmichael, he fought in the three major actions prior to the final assault on the capital city. He must have brought favourable attention to himself during this period because, despite his youth and inexperience, he was promoted Second Corporal on 20 June. Both Smith and Carmichael had ample opportunity to observe the young man at work and in action, and no doubt this explains his inclusion in the

A contemporary sketch of Joshua Grierson which was published in England after his death at Delhi. Presumably the features were based upon a description given by his father.

On 14 December 1981 an event took place at Fatehgarh, 180 miles south-east from Delhi, which stirred many old memories. The occasion was an important one – the presentation of Colours to the Sikh Light Infantry by the President of India, Shri Neelam Sanjiva Reddy. Such a ceremony is a memorable milestone in the history of any regiment but, in the case of the Sikh LI, there were poignant overtones. Born in the heat of the Mutiny, the regiment in its original form served a role which today is quietly ignored by many Indian commentators. The Muzbee Sikhs who fought so well for the British at Delhi were – it might be argued – helping to prolong a foreign domination of their native land. The name 'Delhi' no longer appears on the roll of regimental battle honours. Officially, all mention of those tremendous weeks during the summer of 1857 has been removed from the record. But fighting men the world over take pride in their traditions and the officers and men of the Sikh LI are no exception. Portraits of Duncan Home and Robert Shebbeare still hang in the Officers' Mess at the Regimental Centre. They were the first Commandants and their names are still revered as the founders of the regiment. Consequently, the former British officers of the old pre-1947 Sikh Pioneers and Sikh Light Infantry invited to attend the 1981 ceremony were given an unreserved welcome. An inscribed replica of the Kashmir Gate was given to the representatives of their association who had travelled from New Zealand, Australia, America and Britain to be present that day. Similar replicas were handed over to the commanding officers of each of the sixteen Sikh LI battalions to mark the occasion. Despite the passing of 124 years, despite great changes in the Anglo-Indian relationship, and despite their magnificent services in many later conflicts, the Sikh LI still regard the attack on the Kashmir Gate as the event which epitomises their regimental spirit. The names of Carmichael and Grierson may have been forgotten, but the adventure in which they took part, the triumph which they helped to achieve, lives on in the hearts and minds of those who follow. (Photograph by Adrian Hillier, by kind permission of Major John Hookway)

'explosion party'. In his memoir, John Smith described Joshua as 'Sergeant' Burgess, but we cannot know whether this was a slip of the pen or an unrecorded temporary promotion.

Joshua was one of Philip Salkeld's 'firing party'. After Duncan Home and Robert Hawthorne had laid their bags by the Gate and jumped down into the ditch, and after the shooting of Andrew Carmichael, Philip and Joshua were the only two Europeans left in close proximity to the explosives. Then, when Philip was shot and fell into the ditch, John Smith took his place under the over-hang of the gateway. Unfortunately for Joshua, the mutineers were still firing through the open wicket gate and one of their shots hit him in the body before he could take hold of the box of matches which the Sergeant was holding out to him. Joshua was knocked off balance by the impact of the heavy ball; he started to roll off the bridge and, like his officer, would have fallen ten feet into the ditch if he had not been grabbed by Havildar Tillok Singh. The Havildar

managed to lower Joshua to the floor of the ditch without further injury (despite being himself shot while so doing).

After the explosion, and when the dust had settled, several of the Indian sappers picked up their casualties and took them to the rear to a field hospital. They also carried away the limp body of Joshua Grierson. Shortly afterwards one of them returned to report that both he and Tillok Singh were dead.

Joshua was unmarried at the time of his death and he did not leave a will. His residual estate of 366 rupees (slightly more than £36.00 sterling) was transferred back to Scotland by the military authorities and was handed over to his father, also named Joshua Grierson, at 4 East Arthur Place, Edinburgh.

Andrew Carmichael and Joshua Grierson did not survive to enjoy the tremendous acclaim – in India and Great Britain – which otherwise would have come their way. By the same token, there being no arrangements for posthumous awards, Archdale Wilson could not reward them as he did the four European survivors. Consequently their names have to a certain extent slipped through the net of history; they are the forgotten men of the Kashmir Gate. It is a pity that this should be so. They fought with a valour equal to that of their compatriots and both contributed materially to the success of the operation. But, as happens so often in battle, they chanced to be in the wrong place at the wrong instant in time. By such a slender thread hangs the distinction between obscure mortality and enduring fame.

NOTE

The biographical notes for Carmichael and Grierson (Burgess), and also for Smith (*vide* Appendix G), make reference to the manner in which they were first recruited, attested and inducted. The following background information clarifies the position.

The permanent training depôt of the East India Company was established originally at Newport, on the Isle of Wight, in 1801. In March 1815 it was transferred to Brompton Barracks, Chatham, Kent. In 1842 the War Office asked the HEIC to vacate these barracks because the accommodation was needed for its own (British Army) troops. With great reluctance, the Company transferred its depôt in May 1843 to Warley, near Brentwood in Essex. It remained there until the major re-organisation of 1861.

It was at these depôts that the ordinary artillery and infantry recruits received their introduction to military life. However, during the early weeks, each recruit was assessed with a view to specialist training. Each year, between forty and fifty men were selected at the depôt and chosen as future members of the Sappers & Miners (either Bengal, Bombay or Madras armies). They were required to be 'of good character and abilities', and the minimum educational qualifications were 'a proficiency in reading, writing, spelling and the first four rules of arithmetic'. The chosen men were then sent across the Thames estuary to Chatham to be trained alongside the Queen's sappers for two years under a Lieutenant Colonel, Royal Engineers.

From this it can be seen that John Smith spent eighteen months in basic and engineering training, all of them at Chatham, while Carmichael and Grierson (Burgess) served for several weeks at Warley before transferring to Chatham. They and their contemporaries were the *créme de la créme*, the brightest and the most resourceful. Even a superficial study of the history of the sappers in India reveals the extraordinary achievements of these men who, on many occasions, were given responsibilities which seem almost disproportionate to their junior ranks.

APPENDIX J

The Delhi VCs

Of the total of 182 Victoria Crosses awarded for valour during the Mutiny, forty-three were in respect of military operations in the area of Delhi. By coincidence, they were awarded in almost equal proportion to the two armies involved; twenty-two to officers and men serving with British regiments, and twenty-one to those serving with John Company regiments.

The actions which resulted in these awards were spread over a period of four and a half months. For the convenience of the reader, the following citations have been arranged in groupings which reflect the main phases of the local campaign and which indicate the chronological flow of events.

The first group is very small, but it comprises the names of three men who displayed extraordinary devotion to duty and total disregard for their own safety. They were all employed in a magazine at Delhi at the time when the Mutiny first broke out.

Apart from the main magazine two miles north of the city, Delhi contained a number of ordnance stores. The largest was in the charge of a fat and rather shy young man, Lieutenant George Willoughby, Commissary of Ordnance. When the mutineers from Meerut first reached the capital on 11 May, he immediately understood the importance of denying them access to the weapons and munitions in his care. With the help of his four assistants, Forrest, Raynor, Buckley and Scully, he barred the entrance doors and laid demolition charges. He also armed his men and loaded a cannon with grapeshot.

The Pandis soon tried to force their way in. Willoughby's group of officers and civilian clerks put up a fierce but short-lived resistance. The attackers scaled the boundary walls and swarmed across the rooftops. Willoughby gave the order for Scully to light the fuse. The resultant explosion was heard in Meerut, nearly fifty miles away. Hundreds of mutineers and Indian civilians were killed and injured in the surrounding streets but, as though by a miracle, Scully was the only defender to be killed by the blast. Willoughby, Forrest, Raynor and Buckley all got away from the city safely, although Forrest and Buckley both received gunshot wounds. Sadly, George Willoughby was murdered by villagers a few days later and, there being no provision for posthumous decorations, he went unrewarded. However, his three assistants lived long enough for their gallantry to be reported and officially recognised by the award of the VC.

BUCKLEY, John

Deputy Assistant Commissary, Commissariat Department (Bengal Establishment). Born Stalybridge (Cheshire) 24 May 1813, died London 14 July 1876. Memorials in Tower Hamlets Cemetery and on the Delhi Magazine gateway. *The London Gazette* 18 June 1858, page 2959.

> 'For gallant conduct in the defence of the Magazine at Delhi on 11th May 1857.'

FORREST, George

Lieutenant, Bengal Veteran Establishment. Escaped from Delhi to Meerut with Philip Salkeld (*vide* Appendix F). Born Dublin 1800, died Dehra Dun (India) 3 November 1859. Memorial on the Delhi Magazine gateway. *The London Gazette* 18 June 1858, page 2959.

> 'For gallant conduct in the defence of the Dehli Magazine on 11th May 1857.'

RAYNOR, William

Lieutenant, Bengal Veteran Establishment. Later Captain. Thought to have been the oldest-ever VC winner (aged almost 64 at the time of *The London Gazette* announcement). With Forrest, he was favourably mentioned during the Parliamentary debates on 8 February 1858 (*vide* Appendix D). Born Plumtree (Nottinghamshire) July 1795. Attested in the Bengal Artillery 11 June 1812, age sixteen, but soon transferred to Infantry. Died Ferozepore (India) 13 December 1860 (cause of death 'apoplexia', buried next day in Ferozepore Civil Cemetery). Memorial on the Delhi Magazine gateway. *The London Gazette* 18 June 1858, page 2959.

> 'For gallant conduct in the defence of the Magazine at Delhi on 11th May 1857.'

The second group is by far the largest (comprising the names of twelve British army personnel and four from John Company). These awards were made as a direct result of operations during the period when Anson, Reed and Wilson successively fought their way through to the Ridge, seized it, held it against repeated Pandi sorties, gradually came to dominate the no-man's-land between the Ridge and the city, and then finally prepared for the assault. For convenience, this period may be referred to as 'the siege' but, in practice, this was not a siege in the conventional sense of that word. The Delhi Field Force was much too small to surround the city. It was a partial siege, the attacking force being drawn up in positions facing the short northern wall only. The left flank was covered by the Jumna river, but the right flank was always open to attack and infiltration by the mutineers. Consequently, the long hot summer weeks featured a series of minor and major battles as the Pandis attempted to recapture the Ridge and to interrupt the flow of supplies from Phillaur and Ferozepore.

CADELL, Thomas
Lieutenant, 2nd Bengal European Fusiliers. Later Colonel CB. Cousin of Lieutenant S H Lawrence VC (Lucknow award). Cadell was not recommended until 1861, and his award was then nearly refused on the grounds of lateness. Born Cockenzie (East Lothian) 5 September 1835, died Edinburgh 6 April 1919. *The London Gazette* 29 April 1862, page 2229.

'For having, on the 12th June, 1857, at the flagstaff picquet at Delhi, when the whole of the picquet of Her Majesty's 75th Regiment and 2nd European Bengal Fusiliers were driven in by a large body of the enemy, brought in from amongst the enemy a wounded bugler of his own regiment, under a most severe fire, who would otherwise have been cut up by the rebels. Also, on the same day, when the Fusiliers were retiring, by order, on Metcalfe's house, on its being reported that there was a wounded man left behind, Lieutenant Cadell went back of his own accord towards the enemy, accompanied by three men, and brought in a man of the 75th Regiment, who was severely wounded, under a most heavy fire from the advancing enemy.'

COGHLAN, Cornelius
Colour Sergeant, 75th Regiment. Also appears as Coughlan. The lateness of the award resulted from the CO's failure to submit a formal recommendation. Dates of acts of bravery, 8 June and 18 July 1857. Born Eyrecourt (Co Galway) 27 June 1828, died Westport (Co Mayo) 14 February 1915. *The London Gazette* 11 November 1862, page 5346.

'For gallantly venturing, under a heavy fire, with three others, into a serai occupied by the enemy in great numbers, and removing Private Corbett, 75th Regiment, who lay severely wounded.

Also for cheering and encouraging a party which hesitated to charge down a lane in Subjee Mundee, at Delhi, lined on each side with huts, and raked by a cross-fire; then entering with the said party into an enclosure filled with the enemy, and destroying every man.

For having, also, on the same occasion returned under a cross-fire to collect doolies, and carry off the wounded – a service which was successfully performed, and for which this man obtained great praise from the officers of his regiment.'

DIVANE, John

Private, 60th Rifles. Also appears as Devine. Elected by ballot under Rule 13 of the Royal Warrant. Born Canavane (Co Galway) November 1822, died Penzance (Cornwall) 1 December 1888. *The London Gazette* 20 January 1860, page 178.

> 'For distinguished gallantry in heading a successful charge made by the Baluchi and Sikh troops on one of the enemy's trenches before Delhi, on the 10th of September, 1857. He leaped out of our trenches, closely followed by the native troops, and was shot down from the top of the enemy's breastworks.'

GARVIN, Stephen

Colour Sergeant, 60th Rifles. Born Cashel (Co Tipperary) 1826, died Chesterton (Oxfordshire) 23 November 1874. *The London Gazette* 20 January 1860, page 178.

> 'For daring and gallant conduct before Delhi on the 23rd June, 1857, in volunteering to lead a small party of men, under a heavy fire, to the "Sammy House", for the purpose of dislodging a number of the enemy in position there, who kept up a destructive fire on the advanced battery of heavy guns, in which, after a sharp contest, he succeeded. Also recommended for gallant conduct throughout the operations before Delhi.'

GREEN, Patrick

Private, 75th Regiment. Later Colour Sergeant. Award conferred under Rule 7 by Sir Colin Campbell, C-in-C East Indies, in General Order dated 28 July 1858. Born Ballinasloe (Co Galway) 1824, died Cork (Co Cork) 19 July 1889. *The London Gazette* 26 October 1858, page 4574.

> 'The Commander-in-Chief in India is pleased to approve that the undermentioned soldier be presented, in the name of Her Most Gracious Majesty, with a medal of the Victoria Cross, for valour and daring in the field, viz: Private Patrick Green, Her Majesty's 75th Foot. For having on the 11th September, 1857, when the picquet at the Koodsia Baugh at Delhi was hotly pressed by a large body of the enemy, successfully rescued a comrade who had fallen wounded as a skirmisher.'

HANCOCK, Thomas

Private, 9th Lancers. Later Corporal. Announced jointly with Private John Purcell 9th Lancers. An 'immediate' award under Rule 7 by GOC Delhi Field Force upon the recommendation of Brigadier General J H Grant CB, commanding Cavalry Brigade, and forwarded direct to the War Office by Lord Canning. An unusual and 'irregular' award, because it was not notified first to C-in-C India. Date of action, 19 June 1857. The

British artillerymen beat off a sudden Pandi raid. Throughout the long scorching summer of 1857, prior to the final assault on 14 September, the mutineers made repeated sorties against the batteries and entrenchments constructed on and around the Ridge by the engineers and sappers of the Delhi Field Force. They varied in scale from minor skirmishes in company strength to full scale battles (such as that fought as Najafgarh on 25 August). It was only with great difficulty that the British finally gained control of the 2,000 yards of open ground which separated the Ridge from the city walls - and they never cleared their right flank which was enfiladed by Pandi batteries located outside the city to the south. (India Office Library & Records)

details published in London consisted of an extract from General Grant's report concerning the action fought on 19 June 1857. Hancock was born Kensington (London) July 1823, died London 12 March 1871. *The London Gazette* 15 January 1858, page 178.

> 'The guns, I am happy to say, were saved, but a waggon of Major Scott's battery was blown up. I must not fail to mention the excellent conduct of a Sowar of the 4th Irregular Cavalry, and two men of the 9th Lancers, Privates Thomas Hancock and John Purcell, who, when my horse was shot down, remained by me throughout. One of these men and the Sowar offered me their horses, and I was dragged out by the Sowar's horse. Private Hancock was severely wounded, and Private Purcell's horse was killed under him. The Sowar's name is Roopur Khan.'

HARTIGAN, Henry

Sergeant, 9th Lancers. Appears also as Pensioned Sergeant. Decorated for valour on two separate occasions four months apart. Born Drumlea (Co Fermanagh) March 1826, died Calcutta 29 October 1886. *The London Gazette* 19 June 1860, page 2316.

> 'For daring and distinguished gallantry in the following instances: At the Battle of Budle-Ke-Serai, near Delhi, on the 8th June, 1857, in going to the assistance of Sergeant H. Helstone, who was wounded, dismounted, and surrounded by the enemy, and at the risk of his own life carrying him to the rear.
>
> On the 10th October, 1857, at Agra, in having run unarmed to the assistance of Sergeant Crews, who was attacked by four rebels. Hartigan caught a tulwar from one of them with his right hand, and with the other hit him on the mouth, disarmed him, and then defended himself against the other three, killing one and wounding two, when he was himself disabled from further service by severe and dangerous wounds.'

HILLS, James

Second Lieutenant, Bengal Horse Artillery. Later Lieutenant General Sir James Hills-Johnes GCB. Brother-in-law of Lieutenant W G Cubitt VC. The account published in London is woefully inadequate. Hills defended his battery almost single-handed during an enemy cavalry raid on 9 July 1857. He fought five mutineers with his fists and sword, killing or wounding them all despite being himself slashed across the head. A joint citation with Tombs, his senior officer. Hills was born Neechindpore (India) 20 August 1833, died Dolau-Cothy (Carmarthenshire) 3 January

The 1st (Bengal European) Fusiliers on the march to join the Delhi Field Force. First raised by Clive in 1759 for service against the French dominions in India and composed entirely of white troops, the regiment had already won twenty battle honours to adorn its Colours before the Mutiny of 1857. In May of that year the regiment was stationed at Dagshai, far to the west, on the border with Afghanistan. After a forced march down through the frontier hills, then across the plains of the Indus and the upper Ganges valleys, it arrived in time to take part in the siege and the final assault (gaining another battle honour and two VC awards). Other troops gave the Fusiliers the nickname 'the dirty shirts' as a result of their habit of fighting at Delhi in their shirt-sleeves. Subsequently absorbed into the British army as HM 101st Regiment, then later amalgamated with the 104th Regiment, formerly the 2nd (Bengal European) Fusiliers, the regiment was given the title Royal Munster Fusiliers in 1881 and survived until its disbandment in 1922. (India Office Library & Records)

1919. Memorial in Caio Churchyard, near Dolau-Cothy. His Victoria Cross and other awards have been presented recently to the Royal Artillery Institution by a descendent member of the family. *The London Gazette* 27 April 1858, page 2050.

> 'For very gallant conduct on the part of Lieutenant Hills before Delhi, in defending the position assigned to him in case of alarm, and for noble behaviour on the part of Lieutenant-Colonel Tombs in twice coming to his subaltern's rescue, and on each occasion killing his man.'

JONES, Stowell Alfred

Lieutenant, 9th Lancers. Later Lieutenant Colonel (retired) managing the sewage works Aldershot District. Born Liverpool (Lancashire) 24 June 1832, died Finchampstead (Berkshire) 29 May 1920. *The London Gazette* 18 June 1858, page 2960.

> 'The Cavalry charged the rebels and rode through them. Lieutenant Jones, of the 9th Lancers, with his Squadron, captured one of their guns, killing the drivers, and, with Lieutenant-Colonel Yule's assistance, turned it upon a village, occupied by the rebels, who were quickly dislodged. This was a well-conceived act, gallantly executed.'

McGOVERN, John

Private, 1st Bengal European Fusiliers. Also distinguished himself at Markoul on 16 December 1857 and, twenty-two years later, was recommended for a bar to his VC in respect of that action (refused). Born

Templeport (Co Cavan) 16 May 1825, died Hamilton (Ontario) 22 November 1888. Duplicate medal issued on 10 July 1860 and presented to the Royal Munster Fusiliers Old Comrades' Association in 1922. *The London Gazette* 21 June 1859, page 2420.

'For gallant conduct during the operations before Delhi, but more especially on the 23rd June, 1857, when he carried into camp a wounded comrade under a very heavy fire from the enemy's battery, at the risk of his own life.'

PURCELL, John

Private, 9th Lancers. An 'immediate' award under Rule 7 by GOC Delhi Field Force. Joint citation with Private Thomas Hancock. Purcell died on active service and so the Cross was sent to his brother James. Born Kilcommon (Co Galway) 1814, died Delhi 19 September 1857. *The London Gazette* 15 January 1858, page 178.

SUTTON, William

Bugler, 60th Rifles. Later Sergeant. Elected by ballot under Rule 13 of the Royal Warrant. Subsequently lost his Cross while serving on the permanent staff of the Antrim Militia. Duplicate issued 1872. Born Ightham (Kent) 1830, died Ightham 16 February 1888. Memorial in Ightham Church. *The London Gazette* 20 January 1860, page 178.

'For gallant conduct at Delhi on the 13th of September, 1857, the night previous to the assault, in volunteering to reconnoitre the breach. This soldier's conduct was conspicuous throughout the operations, especially on the 2nd August, 1857, on which occasion, during an attack by the enemy in force, he rushed forward over the trenches and killed one of the enemy's buglers, who was in the act of sounding.'

THOMPSON, James

Private, 60th Rifles. Elected by ballot under Rule 13 of the Royal Warrant. He sold his medals after leaving the army. Later, following his death, his son tried to raise a claim for their return to the family. Thompson was born Yoxall (Staffordshire) 1830, died Walsall (Staffordshire) 5 December 1891. Memorial in the Old Cemetery, Walsall. *The London Gazette* 20 January 1860, page 179.

'For gallant conduct in saving the life of his Captain (Captain Wilton), on the 9th of July, 1857, by dashing forward to his relief when that officer was surrounded by a party of Ghazis, who made a sudden rush on him from a serai, and killing two of them before further assistance could reach [*sic*].

Also recommended for conspicuous conduct throughout the siege. Wounded.'

TOMBS, Henry
Lieutenant Colonel CB, Bengal Artillery. Later Major General KCB. Date of action, 9 July 1857, Delhi Ridge, joint citation with Second Lieutenant James Hills. Tombs shot two mutineers who were attempting to cut down Hills while the latter was engaged in hand-to-hand fighting. He and Hills then pursued an escaping mutineer who fought them with skill and courage. Tombs killed this man with his sword. Born Calcutta 10 November 1825, died Newport (Isle of Wight) 2 August 1876. Memorial in Woolwich Garrison Church (London). *The London Gazette* 27 April 1858, page 2050.

TURNER, Samuel
Private, 60th Rifles. Born Witnesham (Suffolk) February 1826, died Meerut (India) 13 June 1868. After the Mutiny he took his pension and retired to Meerut where he established himself in business as a 'farrier and hotel keeper'. Died prematurely, age 42, cause of death stated to be 'insalitio'. *The London Gazette* 20 January 1860, page 179.

> 'For having, at Delhi, on the night of the 19th of June, 1857, during a severe conflict with the enemy, who attacked the rear of the camp, carried off on his shoulders, under a heavy fire, a mortally wounded officer, Lieutenant Humphreys, of the Indian Service. During this service Private Turner was wounded by a sabre-cut in the right arm. His gallant conduct saved the above-named officer from the fate of the others, whose mangled remains were not recovered until the following day.'

WADESON, Richard
Lieutenant, 75th Regiment. Later Colonel and Lieutenant Governor of the Royal Hospital, Chelsea. Born Lancaster (Lancashire) 31 July 1826, died Chelsea (London) 24 January 1885. Memorial at the Royal Hospital. *The London Gazette* 24 December 1858, page 5518.

> 'For conspicuous bravery at Delhi, on the 18th July, 1857, when the regiment was engaged in the Subjee Mundee, in having saved the life of Private Michael Farrell, when attacked by a Sowar of the enemy's cavalry and killing the Sowar. Also, on the same day, for rescuing Private John Barry, of the same regiment, when, wounded and helpless, he was attacked by a cavalry Sowar, whom Lieutenant Wadeson killed.'

And so we come to the climactic moment in the story of the Delhi Field Force. The events of that momentous day – 14 September – were crucial to the subsequent development of Anglo-Indian history. The British gambled all upon a single throw of the dice. In the event, they succeeded in their aim, but only by the narrowest of margins. Nine Victoria Crosses

Hawthorne VC in his later years, an impression by the American artist Kenneth Petrie.

were awarded for services rendered that day, four of them being to Duncan Home and his companions at the Kashmir Gate.

HAWTHORNE, Robert
Bugler, 52nd Regiment. An 'immediate' award under Rule 7 of the Royal Warrant. See Appendix A and Appendix H for full details. Born Maghera (Co Londonderry) 1822, died Manchester 2 February 1879. *The London Gazette* 27 April 1858, page 2051.

HOME, Duncan Charles
Lieutenant, Bengal Engineers. An 'immediate' award under Rule 7 of the Royal Warrant. See Appendix A and Appendix D for full details. Born Jubbulpore (India) 10 June 1828, died Malagarh (India) 1 October 1857. *The London Gazette* 18 June 1858, page 2961.

McGUIRE, James
Sergeant, 1st Bengal European Fusiliers. VC forfeited by Royal Warrant dated 12 December 1862. This signifies that his name was removed from the official Roll of VC recipients, but he could not be obliged to return his Cross to the authorities. His was the second unfortunate case of only eight such forfeitures in the history of the award. The official reason for this forfeiture was never announced publicly, but the evidence suggests that he had been convicted a short while previously by an Irish court of having stolen a cow from his uncle as recompense for an unpaid debt (McGuire had by then left the army and was working as a farmer). In due course his medals were acquired by a collector, Major A G Moutray, and then sold at auction in 1954. Purchased by the Royal Munster Fusiliers Association, they were presented in 1955 to the Museum of the Disbanded Irish Regiments. In 1960 this museum was incorporated in the collection of the National Army Museum. The medals are now on display in the Irish section of the NAM branch at the Royal Military Academy, Sandhurst. Lamentably, over the years, any accompanying documentation which Moutray might have acquired has been misplaced and cannot at this time be traced. The entire episode raises a number of unanswered questions and is worthy of detailed research. McGuire was born in Enniskillen (Co Fermanagh) in 1827. The date of his death is stated to have been 12 December 1862. However, this is the day on which the Queen signed the forfeiture Warrant. The coincidence of dates raises doubts concerning the accuracy of earlier research work. Perhaps the date of death is stated wrongly, or possibly he committed suicide in a moment of shame and humiliation. *The London Gazette* (award) 24 December 1858, page 5519.

> 'At the assault on Delhi on the 14th September, 1857, when the Brigade had reached the Cabul Gate, the 1st Fusiliers and 75th Regiment and some Sikhs were waiting for orders, and some of the regiments were getting ammunition served out (three boxes of which exploded from some cause not clearly known, and two others were in a state of ignition), when Sergeant McGuire and Drummer Ryan rushed into the burning mass, and seizing the boxes, threw them, one after the other, over the parapet into the water. The confusion consequent on the explosion was very great, and the crowd of soldiers and native followers, who did not know where the danger lay, were rushing into

certain destruction, when Sergeant McGuire and Drummer Ryan, by their coolness and personal daring, saved the lives of many at the risk of their own.'

RYAN, Miles
Drummer, 1st Bengal European Fusiliers. Joint citation with Sergeant James McGuire, referring to the assault on 14 September 1857. Born Londonderry (Ireland) 1826, allegedly died India January 1887 (but this is not supported by the available evidence). *The London Gazette* 24 December 1858, page 5519.

SALKELD, Philip
Lieutenant, Bengal Engineers. See Appendix A and Appendix F for full details. Joint citation with Lieutenant Duncan Home. Born Fontmell Magna (Dorset) 13 October 1830, died Delhi 10 October 1857. *The London Gazette* 18 June 1858, page 2961.

SHEBBEARE, Robert Haydon
Lieutenant (Brevet Captain), 60th Bengal Native Infantry. Born Clapham (London) 13 January 1827, died at sea aboard the SS *Emau* south of Shanghai (China) 16 September 1869. *The London Gazette* 21 October 1859, page 3792.

'For distinguished gallantry at the head of the Guides with the 4th column of assault at Delhi, on the 14th September, 1857, when after twice charging beneath the wall of the loopholed serai, it was found impossible, owing to the murderous fire, to attain the breach. Captain (then Lieutenant) Shebbeare endeavoured to reorganize the men, but one-third of the Europeans having fallen, his efforts to do so failed. He then conducted the rear-guard of the retreat across the canal most successfully. He was most miraculously preserved through the affair, but yet left the field with one bullet through his cheek and a bad scalp wound along the back of the head from another.'

One of the best-known artistic impressions of the Kashmir Gate attack, this sketch was made by the professional artist Eyre Crowe ARA (1824–1910). Crowe never visited India, but based his picture upon details given by his brother-in-law, Colonel Edward Thackeray VC (a friend and contemporary of Home and Salkeld). Two inaccuracies – the inclusion of the tree and the unsealed right-hand portico – indicate that Crowe made use of photographs taken some years after the action. In all other respects, the picture is basically accurate.

SMITH, Henry

Lance Corporal, 52nd Regiment. Later Sergeant. An 'immediate' award under Rule 7 by GOC Delhi Field Force. Born Thames Ditton (Surrey) 1825, died Morar Cantonment (Gwalior, India) 20 August 1862 (cause of death 'cholera spasmodica'). Apparently there is no surviving monument; probably buried in a mass grave during an epidemic. *The London Gazette* 27 April 1858, page 2051.

> 'Lance-Corporal Smith most gallantly carried away a wounded comrade, under a heavy fire of grape and musketry, on the Chaundee Chouck, in the city of Delhi, on the morning of the assault on the 14th September, 1857.'

SMITH, John

Sergeant, Bengal Sappers & Miners. See Appendix A and Appendix G for full details. Born Ticknall (Derbyshire) February 1814, died Jullundur (India) 26 June 1864. *The London Gazette* 27 April 1858, page 2051.

WALLER, George

Colour Sergeant, 60th Rifles. Later Sergeant, Permanent Staff Instructor, 13th Sussex Rifle Volunteers. He took a leading part in the assault despite having been severely wounded in the thigh by gunshot on 19 June. Elected by ballot under Rule 13 of the Royal Warrant. Born West Horsley (Surrey) June 1827, died Cuckfield (Sussex) 10 January 1877. *The London Gazette* 20 January 1860, page 178.

Six elderly but durable VC winners photographed at the Royal Hospital Chelsea, in July 1910. From left to right: Lieutenant General Sir James Hills-Johnes (who won his award as Lieutenant Hills, Bengal Artillery, on the Ridge at Delhi in July 1857); Major General Luke O'Connor (decorated for valour while serving with the 23rd Regiment in the Crimea); Field Marshal Sir Evelyn Wood (a dashing young subaltern of the 'Death or Glory Boys', the 17th Lancers, he twice distinguished himself in single-handed combat with Pandi troops); Field Marshal the Earl Roberts (known throughout the army as 'Bobs', he fought at Delhi and Bolandshahr as Lieutenant Frederick Roberts, Bengal Artillery, and was awarded his Cross for great bravery at Khodagunge in January 1858); Field Marshal Sir George White (decorated for valour as Major White of the 92nd Regiment during the Second Afghan War of 1878–80); and Colonel Sir Edward Thackeray (formerly Lieutenant E T Thackeray, Bengal Engineers, a personal friend of Duncan Home and Philip Salkeld, he extinguished a dangerous fire in the Delhi Magazine on 16 September 1857). The white hair and the splendid finery of exalted rank conceal the fact that each man, in his youth, had engaged in hand-to-hand combat and had killed with the sword. (National Army Musuem)

> 'For conspicuous bravery at Delhi, on the 14th September, 1857, in charging and capturing the enemy's guns near the Cabul Gate; and again, on the 18th of September, 1857, in the repulse of a sudden attack made by the enemy on a gun near the Chandney Chouk.'

The battle to throw the mutineers out of Delhi lasted from 14 to 20 September. The narrowness of the streets prevented extensive use of artillery and cavalry. This was mainly an infantryman's battle, fought at the most primitive hand-to-hand level. No quarter was given on either side, and the majority of the Pandis who died in the battle did so by the cold steel of the bayonet. Only three Victoria Crosses were awarded as a consequence of these six bitter days of conflict. Such a comparatively modest number must be attributed to the fact that so many of the engagements were fought by small parties of infantrymen, grimly clearing the houses room by room, with no officer present to record their services.

READE, Herbert Taylor
Surgeon, 61st Regiment. Later Surgeon General CB and Honorary Surgeon to HM the Queen. His recommendation was delayed by the illness of his CO and frequent changes in the command of the regiment. Born Perth (Upper Canada) 20 September 1828, died Bath (Somerset) 23 June 1897. *The London Gazette* 5 February 1861, page 449.

'During the siege of Delhi, on the 14th September, 1857, while Surgeon

Reade was attending to the wounded, at the end of one of the streets of the city, a party of rebels advanced from the direction of the bank, and having established themselves in the houses in the street, commenced firing from the roofs. The wounded were thus in very great danger, and would have fallen into the hands of the enemy, had not Surgeon Reade drawn his sword, and calling upon the few soldiers who were near to follow, succeeded, under a very heavy fire, in dislodging the rebels from their position.

Surgeon Reade's party consisted of about ten in all, of whom two were killed, and five or six wounded.

Surgeon Reade also accompanied the regiment at the assault of Delhi, and on the morning of the 16th September, 1857, was one of the first up at the breach in the magazine, which was stormed by the 61st Regiment and Belooch Battalion, upon which occasion he, with a sergeant of the 61st Regiment, spiked one of the enemy's guns.'

RENNY, George Albert

Lieutenant, Bengal Horse Artillery. Later Major General. His VC and other medals were stolen from the Suffolk home of a descendant member of his family in 1978. Five years later, in the Spring of 1983, they were discovered abandoned under a pile of mouldering leaves on Sheen Common, near Richmond, London. The finder was an amateur treasure hunter making a routine random search with a metal detector. Born Riga (Russia) 12 May 1827, died Bath (Somerset) 5 January 1887. Grave in Locksbrook Cemetery, Bath. *The London Gazette* 12 April 1859, page 1483.

'Lieutenant-Colonel Farquhar, commanding the 1st Belooch Regiment, reports that he was in command of the troops stationed in the Delhi Magazine, after its capture on the 16th September, 1857. Early in the forenoon of that day, a vigorous attack was made on the post by the enemy, and was kept up with great violence for some time, without the slightest chance of success. Under cover of a heavy cross-fire from the high houses on the right flank of the Magazine, and from Selinghur and the Palace, the enemy advanced to the high wall of the Magazine, and endeavoured to set fire to a thatched roof. The roof was partially set fire to, which was extinguished at the spot by a Sepoy of the Belooch Battalion, a soldier of the 61st Regiment having in vain attempted to do so. The roof having been again set on fire, Captain Renny with great gallantry mounted to the top of the wall of the Magazine, and flung several shells with lighted fuses over into the midst of the enemy, which had an almost immediate effect, as the attack at once became feeble at that point, and soon after ceased there.'

THACKERAY, Edward Albert

Second Lieutenant, Bengal Engineers. Later Colonel KCB FRGS. Cousin of the novelist William Makepeace Thackeray. Born Broxbourne (Hertfordshire) 19 October 1836, died Gerassio (Italy) 3 September 1927 (the last of the Delhi VCs). *The London Gazette* 29 April 1862, page 2229.

> 'For cool intrepidity and characteristic daring in extinguishing a fire in the Delhi magazine enclosure, on the 16th September, 1857, under a close and heavy musketry fire from the enemy, at the imminent risk of his life from the explosion of combustible stores in the shed in which the fire occurred.'

Delhi passed back into the hands of the British. This once beautiful city, packed with valuable artefacts of every description, had been pillaged by mutineers and back-street scavengers in May; now it suffered a second wave of despoilation and looting as the exultant Delhi Field Force tasted the first fruits of victory. For several days following the raising of the Union flag over the Royal Palace, conditions in the capital were chaotic. However, Wilson and his senior staff understood the importance of maintaining the initiative now that they had driven the mutinous troops out into open country. The Force was soon split into a number of smaller groups – 'moveable columns' – which were ordered to pursue the enemy and to dislodge him from his other strongholds.

On 28 September, the column led by Colonel Greathed met the Pandis at the fortified town of Bolandshahr. This clash is one of the many actions fought during the course of the Mutiny which history has ignored, and yet it was conducted with such ferocity that it resulted in the award of six Victoria Crosses. Duncan Home, who was there, described it as 'a tolerably sharp action'. Perhaps his understatement was deliberate, but it was certainly much more than a minor fracas. With six VCs earned in three hours, compared with eleven VCs for the final assault and recapture of Delhi, a battle which lasted six days, Bolandshahr must be regarded as an important event and an appropriate culmination to the Delhi story.

ANSON, The Honourable Augustus Henry Archibald

Captain, 84th Regiment. Later Brevet Lieutenant Colonel. Born Slebech Hall, Pembroke (Wales) 5 March 1835, died Cannes (France) 17 November 1877. Memorial in Lichfield Cathedral. *The London Gazette* 24 December 1858, page 5513.

> 'For conspicuous bravery at Bolundshahur, on the 28th September, 1857. The 9th Light Dragoons [*sic*] had charged through the town, and were reforming in the serai; the enemy attempted to close the entrance by drawing their carts across it, so as to shut in the cavalry and form a cover from which to fire upon them. Captain Anson, taking a lance, dashed out of the gateway, and knocked the drivers off their carts.

Owing to a wound in his left hand, received at Delhi, he could not stop his horse, and rode into the middle of the enemy, who fired a volley at him, one ball passing through his coat. At Lucknow at the assault of the Secundra Bagh, on the 16th November, 1857, he entered with the storming party on the gates being burst open. He had his horse killed, and was himself slightly wounded. He has shown the greatest gallantry on every occasion, and has slain many enemies in fight.'

BLAIR, Robert

Lieutenant, 2nd Dragoon Guards. Later Captain. Cousin of Captain James Blair VC, 32nd Lancers. Born Linlithgow (West Lothian) 13 March 1834, died Cawnpore (India) 28 March 1859. *The London Gazette* 18 June 1858, page 2960.

'A most gallant feat was here performed by Lieutenant Blair, who was ordered to take a party of one sergeant and twelve men and bring in a deserted ammunition waggon. As his party approached, a body of fifty or sixty of the enemy's horse came down upon him from a village, where they had remained unobserved; without a moment's hesitation, he formed up his men, and, regardless of the odds, gallantly led them on, dashing through the rebels. He made good his retreat without losing a man, leaving nine of them dead on the field. Of these he killed four himself; but, to my regret, after having run a native officer through the body with his sword, he was severely wounded, the joint of his shoulder being nearly severed.'

DIAMOND, Bernard

Sergeant, Bengal Horse Artillery. Joint citation with Gunner Richard Fitzgerald. Born Portglenone (Co Armagh) 1827, died Masterton (New Zealand) 24 January 1892. *The London Gazette* 27 April 1858, page 2051.

'For an act of valour performed in action, against the rebels and mutineers at Boolundshur, on the 28th September, 1857, when these two soldiers evinced the most determined bravery in working their gun under a very heavy fire of musketry, whereby they cleared the road of the enemy, after every other man belonging to it had been either killed or disabled by wounds.'

DONOHOE, Patrick

Private, 9th Lancers. Born Nenagh (Co Tipperary) 1830, died Ashbourne (Co Meath) 16 August 1876. *The London Gazette* 24 December 1858, page 5517.

'For having, at Bolundshadur [*sic*], on the 28th September, 1857, gone to the support of Lieutenant Blair, who had been severely wounded, and, with a few other men, brought that officer in safety through a large body of the enemy's cavalry.'

FITZGERALD, Richard
Gunner, Bengal Horse Artillery. Joint citation with Sergeant Bernard Diamond. Born St Finbars (Co Cork) December 1831. In 1861 he made a voluntary transfer to the Royal Artillery (British Army) while still serving in India. It is probable that he returned eventually to the United Kingdom with the RA battery with which he was serving. There is no trace of him in the pension or burial registers for India. Place and date of death unknown, but most probably Ireland. *The London Gazette* 27 April 1858, page 2051.

KELLS, Robert
Lance Corporal, 9th Lancers. Later Trumpet Major and, later still, Sergeant Yeoman of the Guard RVM. Born Meerut (India) 7 April 1832, died London 14 April 1905. *The London Gazette* 24 December 1858, page 5517.

> 'For conspicuous bravery at Bolundshadur [*sic*], on the 18th September, 1857, in defending against a number of the enemy his commanding officer, Captain Drysdale, who was lying in a street with his collar-bone broken, his horse having been disabled by a shot, and remaining with him until out of danger.'

ROBERTS, James Reynolds
Private, 9th Lancers. He also appears as J I R Roberts. He died shortly before his Cross could be presented to him. It was sent to his brother Edward, of Barnet Wood, Bromley, Kent, on 21 September 1859. Born Bow (London) 1826, died Marylebone (London) 1 August 1859. *The London Gazette* 24 December 1858, page 5517.

> 'For conspicuous gallantry at Bolundshadur [*sic*], on the 28th September, 1857, in bringing a comrade, mortally wounded, through a street under a heavy musketry fire, in which service he was himself wounded.'

The final group of awards listed here – five in number – is composed of citations which reflect gallant conduct at later actions, but which also encompass previous courageous services at Delhi, or which reflect various acts of bravery in more than one phase of the siege and battle.

GOUGH, Charles John Stanley
Major, 5th Bengal European Cavalry. Later General GCB. The brother of Lieutenant Hugh Gough VC, one of the officers who rescued Philip Salkeld and the other fugitives at Hurchundpore. C J S Gough was born Chittagong (India) 28 January 1832, died Clonmel (Co Tipperary) 6 September 1912. *The London Gazette* 21 October 1859, page 3792.

> 'First, for gallantry in an affair at Khurkowdah, near Rhotuck, on the 15th August, 1857, in which he saved his brother, who was wounded, and killed two of the enemy. Secondly, for gallantry on the 18th

August, when he led a troop of the Guides Cavalry in a charge, and cut down two of the enemy's sowars, with one of whom he had a desperate hand-to-hand combat. Thirdly, for gallantry on the 27th January, 1858, at Shumshabad, where, in a charge, he attacked one of the enemy's leaders, and pierced him with his sword, which was carried out of his hand in the melée. He defended himself with his revolver, and shot two of the enemy. Fourthly, for gallantry on the 23rd February, at Meangunge, where he came to the assistance of Brevet Major O. H. St. George Anson, and killed his opponent, immediately afterwards cutting down another of the enemy in the same gallant manner.'

HEATHCOTE, Alfred Spencer
Lieutenant, 60th Rifles. Later Captain. Elected by ballot under Rule 13 of the Royal Warrant. Born London 29 March 1832, died Bowral (NSW Australia) 21 February 1912. Memorial in St James' Church, Sydney (NSW). *The London Gazette* 20 January 1860, page 178.

'For highly gallant and daring conduct at Delhi throughout the siege, from June to September, 1857, during which he was wounded. He volunteered for services of extreme danger, especially during the six days of severe fighting in the streets after the assault. Elected by the officers of his Regiment.'

PHILLIPPS, Everard Aloysius Lisle
Ensign, 11th Bengal Native Infantry. Recommended under the normal procedure, but killed in action before the Queen could approve the award. Unlike Home and Salkeld (who were recommended under Rule 7), he was ineligible and the medal could not be issued. His was one of the cases which were the subject of discussion in 1906 when representations were made to King Edward VII for the approval of certain retroactive posthumous awards. The whole subject generated a great volume of correspondence and the names of Home and Salkeld were frequently cited (not always in the correct context). The King eventually approved six retroactive awards, including Phillipps, and the Cross was sent to his surviving brother Edward, of Charnwood Lodge, Coalville, Leicester, in February 1907 (50 years after the act for which it was the recognition). Phillipps was born at Grace Dieu Manor (Leicestershire) 28 May 1835, died Delhi 18 September 1857. Memorial at Oscott College (near Birmingham). First *London Gazette* entry (as a Memorandum) 21 October 1859.

'Ensign Everard Aloysius Lisle Phillipps of the 11th Regiment of Bengal Native Infantry, would have been recommended to Her Majesty for decoration of the Victoria Cross, had he survived, for many gallant deeds which he performed during the Siege of Delhi, during which he was wounded three times. At the assault of that city he captured the

Water Bastion, with a small party of men; and was finally killed in the streets of Delhi on the 18th September.'

Second *London Gazette* entry (announcing the award) 15 January 1907, page 325.

'The King has been graciously pleased to approve the Decoration of the Victoria Cross to the undermentioned Officers and men who fell in the performance of acts of valour, and with reference to whom it was notified in the London Gazette that they would have been recommended to Her late Majesty for the Victoria Cross had they survived.'

This second entry is accompanied by details of his original act of gallantry. It also provides similar confirmation of the other five posthumous awards which had been approved by the King.

PROBYN, Dighton MacNaghton

Captain, 2nd Punjab Cavalry. Later General GCB GCSI GCVO ISO. For nearly 50 years he was a member of the Royal Household. Comptroller to the Prince of Wales 1877–91, Keeper of the King's Privy Purse 1901–10, Comptroller to Queen Alexandra 1910–24. Born Marylebone (London) 21 January 1833, died Sandringham (Norfolk) 20 June 1924. Memorial in Sandringham Church. *The London Gazette* 18 June 1858, page 2960.

'Has been distinguished for gallantry and daring throughout this campaign. At the Battle of Agra, when his squadron charged the rebel infantry, he was some time separated from his men, and surrounded by five or six sepoys. He defended himself from the various cuts made at him, and, before his own men had joined him, had cut down two of his assailants. At another time, in single combat with a sepoy, he was wounded in the wrist by the bayonet, and his horse also slightly wounded; but, though the sepoy fought desperately, he cut him down. The same day he singled out a standard-bearer, and, in the presence of a number of the enemy, killed him and captured the standard. These are only a few of the gallant deeds of this brave young officer.'

ROBERTS, Frederick Sleigh

Lieutenant, Bengal Artillery. Later Field Marshal KG KP GCB OM GCSI GCIE VD, one of Great Britain's most illustrious soldiers. Father of Lieutenant Frederick Hugh Sherston Roberts VC, King's Royal Rifle Corps, wounded during an attempt to save twelve 15-pounder guns from the Boers at Colenso on 15 December 1899 and died two days later (six VCs were awarded for this action). Roberts (senior) distinguished himself repeatedly before and during the assault on Delhi and again at Bolandshahr. Finally decorated after yet another act of valour several weeks later. Born Cawnpore (India) 30 September 1832, died on active service while visiting the Indian Corps in France 14 November 1914 at the age of eighty-two. *The London Gazette* 24 December 1858, page 5516.

> 'Lieutenant Roberts's gallantry has on every occasion been most marked. On following up the retreating enemy on the 2nd January, 1858, at Khodagunge, he saw in the distance two Sepoys going away with a standard. Lieutenant Roberts put spurs to his horse, and overtook them just as they were about to enter a village. They immediately turned round, and presented their muskets at him, and one of the men pulled the trigger, but fortunately the caps snapped, and the standard-bearer was cut down by this gallant young officer, and the standard taken possession of by him. He also, on the same day, cut down another Sepoy, who was standing at bay with musket and bayonet, keeping off a Sowar. Lieutenant Roberts rode to the assistance of the horseman, and, rushing at the Sepoy, with one blow of his sword cut him across the face, killing him on the spot.'

An analysis of these awards reveals details which are of interest to the historian. First, we find that forty-five per cent of the Delhi VCs were won by born-and-bred Irishmen. This fact reflects the heavy dependence of the British and John Company armies upon recruitment from the rural areas of Ireland. By the same token, Ireland was obliged to these armies as an outlet for her surplus sons. Poverty and land starvation offered a poor prospect for them in their home country and, given the Irishman's traditional attitudes to life (a willingness to fight and a reluctance to marry), the recruiting sergeants played a valuable role in maintaining an economic and social stability within the Irish working classes.

Secondly, we find that VCs were awarded to officers and men of twelve different regiments and corps, but that two British regiments in particular stand out from the others. The 60th Rifles (later The King's Royal Rifle Corps) won eight Crosses, and the 9th Lancers (or Queen's Royal Lancers) won seven. The Bengal Horse Artillery were also to the forefront with four VCs (and two more went to the Bengal Artillery).

Further analysis shows that it was the British regiments which won most of the VCs awarded for the siege phase, but the majority of awards for the assault and street battle went to John Company personnel. This is a statistical anomaly rather than a yardstick of courage or activity.

Fourthly, there is a surprising uniformity to the ages of the Delhi VC winners. Almost all were in their late twenties or early thirties. Leaving aside the three elderly ordnance experts who so courageously blew up the magazine on 11 May, the average age of the decorated men was 29 (the youngest being 21 and the oldest 43). In other words, these were not carefree hot-headed youngsters in search of fame and glory. To the contrary, they were mature and experienced professional soldiers who well knew the risks they ran. They fought with the power of conviction in the rights of their cause.

Battles of the Mutiny

The suppression of the Mutiny witnessed two major British military operations – the reoccupation of first Delhi and then Lucknow. Too often it is forgotten that a great many other actions took place during that period. Fought over an area the size of Europe, they varied in scale from minor skirmishes to full-pitched battles involving thousands of men. The following pages list some of those actions which, by virtue of the numbers involved and the losses inflicted, may be described as battles in the fullest sense.

A feature of these episodes is the disproportinate strength of the opposing sides. Time and again the British confronted – and defeated – rebel forces many times more numerous than themselves. Certain factors should be borne in mind when considering the figures. First, the British were armed mainly with Enfield and Minié rifles, their opponents with Brown Bess muskets, matchlocks and swords. Secondly, the British leaders were better trained and had more experience of handling military formations in the field. Thirdly, the rebel forces were motivated by an increasingly desperate fear of impending retribution, the British by a furious determination to avenge the alleged atrocities against their womenfolk and children. The passage of time was to prove which of these factors was the most potent.

GHAZI-UD-DIN (Oudh), 30 May, 1857: the Meerut column batters a Pandi force while on the road to Delhi.

HINDUN BRIDGE (Oudh), 31 May 1857: the Meerut column bursts through a second Pandi blocking force.

CAWNPORE (Oudh) (1st battle), 6 June, 1857: Sir Hugh Wheeler, with 240 men, tries to defend 375 civilians from Nana Sahib's 3,000 besieging troops. After three weeks of brave resistance he surrenders. All but 200 European women and children are treacherously murdered (including Wheeler).

BADLI-KI-SERAI (Oudh), 8 June 1857: the Delhi Field Force smashes the last major obstacle on the approach to Delhi.

CHINHUT (Oudh), 30 June 1857: Sir Henry Lawrence, with 300 men and ten guns, sorties from Lucknow to engage Barhat Ahmedi's 6,300 men and sixteen guns. The British are trounced, the long siege of the Residency commences.

SASSIAH (Oudh), 5 July 1857: a Pandi force of 4,000 infantry, 1,500 cavalry and eleven guns advances upon Agra. The city contains many European residents and refugees. Brigadier Polwhele sorties out with 700 British and Indian troops. After a severe action the Pandis are driven off and diverted to Delhi.

TRIMOO GHAT (Punjab) (1st battle), 11 July 1857: Pandis from Sialkot are marching to Gurdespore. Nicholson's moveable column catches them crossing the Ravi river. The Pandis are defeated, losing 400 dead, but Nicholson has no cavalry and so cannot force a conclusion.

FATEHPORE (Oudh), 12 July 1857: Sir Henry Havelock, with 1,100 men and eight guns, is marching from Allahabad to Cawnpore. He clashes with 3,000 Pandis with twelve guns, routs them and continues his march.

AONG (Oudh), 15 July 1857: Havelock meets another rebel force blocking the road to Cawnpore. He defeats 3,000 entrenched Pandis and marches on.

PANDU NADI (Oudh), 15 July 1857: that same evening, Havelock storms across the Pandu Nadi river bridge defended by 2,000 Pandis. News of his success causes Nana Sahib to slaughter the remaining 200 women and children at Cawnpore. The atrocity outrages public opinion around the world and inflames the British soldiery.

MAHARAJPORE (Oudh), 16 July 1857: seven miles from Cawnpore, Havelock's men storm through Nana Sahib's batteries and – too late to save the civilians – recapture the city. Despite disease and heat exhaustion, the British have marched 126 miles in nine days and fought four major actions.

TRIMOO GHAT (Punjab) (2nd battle), 16 July 1857: Pandi forces surviving from the earlier action (12 July) have fortified an island on the Ravi river. The 52nd Regt, led by Nicholson, makes a surprise dawn landing and destroys the rebel force.

ARRAH (Lower Provinces), 25 July 1857: fifteen European and Eurasian residents, with seventy-five loyal Sikhs, fortify themselves in a house and defy 5,000 besieging Pandis. A British relief force from Dinapore is decimated. A second relief column, led by Maj Vincent Eyre, fights through to raise the siege on 3 August.

UNAO (Oudh), 29 July 1857: Henry Havelock leaves 300 men to garrison Cawnpore and departs for Lucknow with 1,500 men and ten guns. After eight miles of march he encounters a road-block of 6,000 Pandis with twenty guns. British infantry make a frontal attack, burst through and march on.

BASHIRATGANJ (Oudh) (1st battle), 29 July 1857: seven miles more and another road-block, with 2,000 rebels, faces Havelock. He outflanks the enemy and routs them. Casualties and disease have reduced his strength to 900 men, so he returns to Cawnpore.

BASHIRATGANJ (Oudh) (2nd battle), 4 August 1857: Havelock again forces a way through, but is obliged by an outbreak of cholera to halt and rest his small force.

BASHIRATGANJ (Oudh) (3rd battle), 12 August 1857: the final destruction of the enemy block-force. The 78th Highlanders and Madras Fusiliers storm the earthworks with the bayonet.

JAGDISPORE (Oudh), 12 August 1857: the forces of a rebel leader, Kunwar Singh, are defeated by Vincent Eyre's column.

BITHUR (Oudh), 16 August 1857: Henry Havelock, outnumbered four-to-one, disperses yet another Pandi force near Cawnpore.

NAJAFGARH (Oudh), 25 August 1857: Nicholson defeats a large sortie by the defenders of Delhi.

PALI (Oudh), 8 September 1857: the army of the Maharajah of Jodhpore – who has sided with the British – is surprised and destroyed by rebel forces.

KUNDAPATI (Oudh), 11 September 1857: Vincent Eyre traps a rebel division boarding barges on the Ganges river. Hundreds of Pandis are shot by British riflemen while trying to swim to safety.

DELHI (Oudh), 14 September 1857: the attack on the Kashmir Gate signals the final assault. John Nicholson is killed in action.

MANDURI (Oudh), 19 September 1857: the first battle fought by Nepalese Crown forces as allies of the British. In two days, 1,200 Gurkhas march fifty miles and then, in ten minutes of ferocious fighting, destroy a larger Pandi force.

The rebels lose 200 dead, the Gurkhas two dead and twenty-six wounded.

MANGALWAR (Oudh), 21 September 1857: Havelock's relief force routs yet another Pandi division blocking the road to Lucknow.

ALAMBAGH (Oudh), 23 September 1857: Havelock reaches the outskirts of Lucknow. After heavy losses his men fight their way through to join the defenders of the Residency. General James Neill is killed in action.

BOLANDSHAHR (Oudh), 28 September 1857: Colonel Greathed's column recaptures this rebel stronghold. Six VCs won.

CHATRA (Chutia Nagpur), 2 October 1857: 180 men of the 53rd Regt, with 150 loyal Sikhs, defeat 3,000 Pandis while guarding the Grand Trunk Road.

AKBARPORE (Oudh), 7 October 1857: Rattray's Sikhs defeat numerous rebels threatening Havelock's line of communication between Allahabad and Lucknow.

AGRA (Oudh), 10 October 1857: Col Greathed's column is surprised in camp, heavily attacked, but quickly reacts and drives off a superior Pandi force. The 9th Lancers and Hodson's Horse are prominent in the action.

KUDYA (Oudh), 19 October 1857: a second rebel defeat at the hands of the Gurkhas.

DHAR (Malwa, Central India), 22 October 1857: the British besiege the fort of a dissident Rajah. After nine days of bombardment the enemy break and run.

CHANDAR (Oudh), 30 October 1857: 1,100 Gurkhas with two guns defeat 4,500 Pandis with seven guns. The men from Nepal – on loan to the British from their own sovereign – enhance their reputation as ferocious fighters.

KAJWA (Oudh), 1 November 1857: 530 men, including a Royal Navy contingent, defeat a large force blocking the road from Fatehpore to Lucknow. Capt William Peel RN assumes command when Col Powell is killed in action. The British lose ninety-five dead, the Pandis 300.

DANCHUA (Oudh), 6 November 1857: Rattray's Sikhs fight a furious battle with the mutinied 32nd Native Infantry.

RAWAL (Malwa, Central India), 12 November 1857: five British officers charge at the head of three regiments of the Nizam of Hyderabad's cavalry against a Pandi column. There are heavy losses on both sides.

NARNUL (Oudh), 16 November 1857: while clearing the area between Agra and Lucknow, two large cavalry brigades clash in pitched battle. The Pandis fight with outstanding courage, but lose the day.

GORARIA (Gwalior, Central India), 23 November 1857: Sir Henry Durand, with 1,500 men and nine guns, destroys a Pandi force of 15,000 men and sixteen guns. The rebel leader in Central India, Firuz Shah, is obliged to evacuate Mandisur.

CAWNPORE (Oudh) (2nd battle), 26 November 1857: 20,000 rebels, under Tantia Topi, advance upon Cawnpore from Gwalior. Sir Charles Windham sorties out and soon meets their advance guard. The British lose 300 dead, are defeated and driven back into their own lines.

CAWNPORE (Oudh) (3rd battle), 6 December 1857: Sir Colin Campbell has arrived with his veterans from the Crimea war. He prepares carefully and then assaults the armies of Nana Sahib and Tantia Topi on the nearby plain. The rebels are driven from the field and the way is open for the relief of Lucknow.

PATIALI (Oudh), 17 December 1857: while clearing the Gangetic Doab, British cavalry charge a strong rebel force, killing 600.

SOBANPORE (Bihar), 26 December 1857: a force of Royal Marines, Royal Navy gunners and Gurkha soldiers defeat 5,200 Pandis and rebel adventurers.

KALI NADI BRIDGE (Oudh), 2 January 1858: the 9th Lancers, 53rd Regt, 93rd Regt and Royal Navy gunners destroy a large Pandi brigade.

PALAMAU (Chutia Nagpur), 21 January 1858: an English officer, with a scratch force of loyal sepoys and irregular levies, captures the village and defeats the local rebel leader.

NASRATPUR (Oudh), 23 January 1858: near Allahabad, British, Indian and Gurkha troops storm a rebel stronghold. The enemy panic and run.

SHAMSABAD (Oudh), 27 January 1858: a British force, under Col Adrian Hope, breaks a Pandi force. The survivors run away but are cut down in large numbers by the 9th Lancers and Hodson's Horse.

SAUGOR (Malwa, Central India), 3 February 1858: Sir Hugh Rose, with 4,500 troops, fights his way through 8,000 troops of the Rajah of Bahpur's army to raise the siege of Saugor. He rescues 170 European women and children.

CHANDA (Oudh), 19 February 1858: 8,000 rebels, armed with matchlocks and tulwars, are routed by a force of 1,800 British and Gurkha troops armed with Enfield rifles.

HAMIDPORE (Oudh), 19 February 1858: the victors of Chanda meet an even larger force, led by the rebel Mehndi Hussein, and disperse it with hardly a shot fired. The dissidents have developed a great fear of being bayonet charged.

PHULPORE (Oudh), 22 February 1858: Gurkhas, British troops, civilian volunteers and naval gunners recapture the town.

BADSHAHGANJ (Oudh), 23 February 1858: a strongly entrenched rebel army, with heavy artillery, is out-witted and destroyed. The British continue their advance towards Lucknow.

MADANPORE (Bandalkhand, Central India), 3 March 1858: Sir Hugh Rose, with John Company troops and the 14th Lt Dragoons, storms the pass at Malthon on the road to Jhansi.

AMHORA (Oudh), 5 March 1858: 14,000 rebels and mutinied sepoys attack a small British mixed force on the approach to Lucknow. The rebels are driven off, losing 400 dead and eight guns.

MUSA BAGH (Oudh), 19 March 1858: Sir James Outram, with 4,000 men, clears the final approaches to Lucknow. He defeats 10,000 rebels under the Begum of Oudh. British cavalry are not ordered forward to exploit the success of the infantry.

LUCKNOW (Oudh), 21 March 1858: the 93rd Highlanders and 4th Punjab Rifles destroy the last remaining stronghold in the centre of the city.

JHANSI (Bandalkhand, Central India), 21 March 1858: Sir Hugh Rose, with 4,500 men, besieges the fortress of the Rani of Jhansi defended by 11,000 rebels. On 5 April he storms the walls but the Rani escapes. 5,000 rebels die, 343 British are killed or wounded.

KOTAH SERAI (Rajputana), 25 March 1858: Maj Gen H G Roberts, with the 83rd and 95th Regts, scatters a rebel force and captures fifty guns.

BETWA (Bandalkhand, Central India), 1 April 1858: Sir Hugh Rose leaves Jhansi to head off Tantia Topi who is coming to support the Rani with 22,000 men. With only 1,500 men of his own, Rose drives his enemy from the field in total confusion.

AZAMGHUR (Oudh), 6 April 1858: while clearing the road from Allahabad to Benares, Lord Mark Kerr smashes through a powerful roadblock of 4,000 Pandis. A brilliant action.

KANKAR (Oudh), 7 April 1858: 1,300 British clear several villages, killing 250 mutineers.

TIGRA (Bihar), 10 April 1858: Sir Edward Lugard's cavalry attack 3,000 rebels, killing eighty.

RUIYAH (Rohilkhand), 15 April 1858: the rebel leader Nirpat Singh inflicts heavy losses on a British force which unsuccessfully attacks his fortifications. Five VCs awarded. Brig Gen Adrian Hope is killed in action.

BHOGNIWALA (Oudh), 17 April 1858: Col John Coke's cavalry charge a rebel position in thick jungle, killing so many that years later the place is reputed to be haunted by their ghosts.

BANDAH (Oudh), 19 April 1858: defeat of the rebel Nawab of Bandah. His army of 7,000 loses 500 killed.

NAGHINA (Rohilkhand), 21 April 1858: 12,000 rebels with fifteen guns are shattered after a day-long series of clashes. The 60th Rifles and 1st Punjab Rifles are prominent.

JAGDISPORE (Bihar), 23 April 1858: the elderly Kunwar Singh, with only 2,000 badly armed villagers at his command, inflicts bloody defeat on a British force. The leader, Capt Le Grand RN, is killed, also nineteen sailors and 102 men of the 35th Regt.

BAREILLY (Rohilkhand), 5 May 1858: Sir Colin Campbell, with a large force, recaptures the city after a battle with the rebel leader Khan Bahadur Khan, but fails to inflict a decisive defeat upon him.

KUNCH (Bandalkhand, Central India), 6 May 1858: between Kalpi and Jhansi, Sir Hugh Rose brings a powerful division against the armies of Tantia Topi and the Rani of Jhansi. The rebels fight bravely but then run.

KOPULDRUG (Bombay Province), 2 June 1858: the rebel leader Bhim Rao is killed and his men driven from their fortress. Fugitives, they are hunted down by British officials with Portuguese troops from Goa. Captured rebels are deported to Portuguese Timor!

HARHA (Oudh), 9 June 1858: the rebel Mohammed Hussein, with 4,000 men, is defeated by a force of sailors and marines. Nine days later he is beaten again.

MORAR (Bandalkhand, Central India), 16 June 1858: near Gwalior, Sir Hugh Rose with 4,000 men fights a close-quarter battle with Tantia Topi's army of 8,000. The 71st Highlanders take heavy losses, the 14th Lt Dragoons take revenge with the sabre.

GWALIOR (Bandalkhand, Central India), 17 June 1858: Sir Hugh Rose, with 5,000 troops, attacks and then storms the massive fortress defended by 10,000 rebels under Tantia Topi and the Rani of Jhansi. The leaders escape and their armies are dispersed.

JAURA ALIPORE (Bandalkhand, Central India), 21 June 1858: cavalry and horse artillery led by Gen Robert Napier overtake the rebels escaping from Gwalior. Tantia Topi's men stand and fight, losing 350 dead, but then break under a cavalry charge.

SANGANIR (Bandalkhand, Central India), 7 August 1858: the fleeing Tantia Topi's battered army is again brought to battle, but again escapes destruction.

KANKRAULI (Nagpur, Central India), 14 August 1858: once more the British overtake Tantia Topi and force him to fight. Once more he is able to slip away, the British lacking sufficient cavalry to encircle his position.

NURIAH (Rohilkhand), 29 August 1858: units of cavalry and 24th Pioneers successfully defend the village against a fanatical rebel attack.

SIRPURAH (Rohilkhand), 30 August 1858: Capt Sam Browne wins his VC – and loses his left arm – while leading cavalry against a gun emplacement. The rebels lose 300 dead and four guns.

MIANGANJ (Oudh), 5 October 1858: between Lucknow and Cawnpore, 200 mutineers are killed and two guns captured.

PANU (Oudh), 6 October 1858: 12,000 rebels with twelve guns, led by Havishand, are defeated by a small force of Queen's Bays and the 88th Regt, with Indian police support. Lt Green of the Rifle Brigade is wounded thirteen times and his arm is cut off, but he fights on.

SHAHJANPORE (Oudh), 8 October 1858: Sir Thomas Seaton intercepts a rebel force, killing 300 and capturing three guns.

1859: a series of minor mopping-up battles result from the British policy of continuing to pursue the demoralised and fragmented rebel groups fleeing for cover in jungle country. Most of the rebellion's leaders are killed, captured or driven into exile. Effective control of the country is restored to British hands.

This list – which is neither complete nor analytical – serves to illustrate the potential for further research. It also demonstrates the difficulty of attempting to catalogue all the regiments present at each action. Many battles were fought by composite units. Battalions which had not been at full strength even at the commencement of the campaign were soon reduced, by death, wounds, heat stroke, cholera, fever and sheer exhaustion, to token numbers. It is to their credit that they unswervingly maintained their fighting spirit and regimental pride.

Selected Bibliography and Sources

The Sikhs and the Sikh Wars
Gen Sir Charles Gough and Arthur D Innes
A D Innes & Company, London 1897

The Sikh Wars 1845–6 and 1848–9
H C B Cook
Leo Cooper Limited, London 1975

History of the Indian Mutiny
T Rice Holmes
MacMillan & Company, London 1898

Eight Month's Campaign
against the Bengal sepoy army during the mutiny of 1857
Col George Bourchier
Smith Elder & Company, London 1858

History of the Indian Mutiny
Kaye & Malleson
Longmans Green & Company, London 1880–1911

The Punjab and Delhi in 1857
Rev J Cave-Brown MA
William Blackwood & Sons, London 1861

The Indian Mutiny
John Harris (edited Ludovic Kennedy)
Book Club Associates, London 1973

The Great Mutiny – India 1857
Christopher Hibbert
Allen Lane – Penguin Books Limited, London 1978

The Sepoy Mutiny as seen by a Subaltern
Colonel Edward Vibart
Smith Elder & Company, London 1898

An Unrecorded Chapter of the Indian Mutiny
Reginald J Wilberforce
John Murray, London 1895

Old Memories
General Sir Hugh Gough GCB VC
William Blackwood & Sons, Edinburgh and London 1897

Two Native Narratives of the Mutiny in Delhi
translated by Sir Theophilus Metcalfe CSI
Constable, London 1898

The Indian Mutiny 1857–58
letters and despatches, Military Dept, Govt of India Vol I
Military Department Press, Calcutta 1893

Two Monsoons
Theon Wilkinson
Gerald Duckworth & Company Limited, London 1976

Crown Imperial – A Corner of Some Foreign Field
Major Alan Harfield
Picton Print (Chippenham) Limited, Chippenham 1981

British Smooth-bore Artillery
Major General B P Hughes CB CBE
Arms & Armour Press, London 1969

The History of the Sikh Pioneers
Lt Gen Sir George MacMunn
Sampson Low Marston & Company, London (nd)

The Indian Sappers & Miners
Lt Col E W C Sandes
The Institution of Royal Engineers. Chatham 1948

The VC and DSO
Sir O'Moore Creagh and E M Humphris
Standard Art Book Company Limited, London (nd)

The Victoria Crosses and George Crosses
of the Honourable East India Company and Indian Army 1856–1945
National Army Museum 1962

British Battles & Medals
Major L L Gordon
Spink & Sons Limited, London 1979

British Gallantry Awards
Abbott & Tamplin
Nimrod Dix & Company, London 1981

The Evolution of the Victoria Cross
M J Crook
Midas Books/Ogilby Trusts, Tunbridge Wells 1975

The Victoria Cross Register
Public Records Office, Kew, Surrey

The Register of the Victoria Cross
This England Books, Cheltenham 1981

The Victoria Cross files (MSS)
Canon W M Lummis MC
Military History Society and National Army Museum

The London Gazette
published by authority, various dates

Hansard's Parliamentary Debates
Third series, Vol 148, 3 Dec 1857 – 22 Feb 1858
Cornelius Buck, London 1858

Biographical Notices of Officers of the Royal (Bengal) Engineers
Edward T Thackeray, London 1900

A List of Inscriptions on Christian Tombs and Monuments in the Punjab (including Delhi), the North West Frontier Province, Kashmir and Afghanistan (with biographical notes)
Miles Irving
Lahore 1910

Original Sources:
Military Estate Papers, Bengal Army – IOR L/AG/34/40/1–104
Cadet Papers of EIC Officers, 1789–1860 – IOR L/MIL/9/107–254
Bengal Service Army Lists, 1770–1858 – IOR L/MIL/10/20–69
General Orders, Bengal Army 1820–1903 – IOR L/MIL/17/2/269–352
Returns of Baptisms; Marriages and Burials for Northern India – IOR N/1

Index

Notes:
(a) in most cases the ranks shown are those held at the time of the events described,
(b) page numbers shown in italics refer to entries in captions.